SO-DJY-804

A PHILOSOPHER REPORTS TO PLANET EARTH

VOLUME ONE

8 AUGUST 2013

To Ken and Mona,

our friends.

Ross Channing Reed

A PHILOSOPHER REPORTS TO PLANET EARTH

VOLUME ONE

ROSS CHANNING REED,
Ph.D.

OzarkMountainWritersGuild

Copyright ©2013 BY ROSS CHANNING REED, Ph.D.

All rights reserved. No part of this book may be reproduced, stored in a retrieval system, or transmitted in any form or by any means, including mechanical, electronic, photocopying, recording, or otherwise, without prior written permission of the publisher.

LIBRARY OF CONGRESS CONTROL NUMBER: 2013946550

ISBN – 13: 978-1-940514-00-0
ISBN – 10: 1940514002

Ozark Mountain Writers Guild
Salem, Missouri 65560

Also by Ross Channing Reed

Love and Death: An Existential Theory of Addiction (2009)

The Terror of the Simulacra trilogy (forthcoming)

Praise for *The Terror of the Simulacra*

"Reed put the stench back in existentialism."
- G. S.

"This book should never have been written,
but... here it is."
- C. W.

"I've seen worse."
- B. A.

"There's a little something here to disappoint
everyone."
- J. R.

"Why?"
- N. J.

" A Derridian-Lacanian-Foucaultian-
Sartrean deconstruction of the
polysemantic valences that pass for the
substantive constructs of our postmodern
society. Nice."
- A. K.

"If you think you know what terrorism is all
about, you need to read this book. If you don't
have a clue about terrorism, you need to read
this book. If you don't like to read, have

somebody read it to you. If you don't know anyone who can read past the 8th grade level, welcome to the United States of America."
- G. M.

"Reminds one of Tolstoy's *War and Peace*, only without the peace."
- D. C.

"Kafka, Sartre, Camus, Dostoevsky, Reed? Whatever."
- P. G.

"If you can read through all this crap, what you get is...more crap. But it's the kind of crap that's worth it."
- S. M.

"A heinous tome."
- K. L.
-

"After reading this, I'm going back on my meds."
- V. N.

"Good enough...I mean bad enough to be banned."
- S. K.

"The modern day *Catcher in the Rye*. Let's call it *The Pitcher in the Pumpernickel*."
- J. J.

"American philosopher Ross Reed has written a poignant, necessary and timeless work. Monica LeBlanc will soon be, without a doubt, part of our cultural unconscious... LeBlanc is the new black."
- J. H.

"What? Reading is for sissies."
- M. M.

"I haven't read a novel since, well, probably the 80s. I did skip to the end and read the last 100 pages of Reed's third volume and they were fantastic. I might even go back and read the rest."
- M. N.

"Demasiada cordura puede ser la peor de las locuras, ver la vida como es y no como debe ser."

Too much common sense can be the worst form of madness, to see life as it is and not as it should be.

Miguel de Cervantes Saavedra, *Don Quixote* (trans. Amanda L. Irwin)

CONTENTS

INTRODUCTION

Scientists discovered the "God particle" (Higgs boson) a year ago, and so far not much has changed.[1] Now, they're searching for dark matter.[2] Regarding dark matter, Amber Hunt writes, "Scientists know dark matter exists by its gravitational pull but, unlike regular matter and antimatter, it's so far been undetectable. Regular matter accounts for about 4 percent of the universe's mass, and dark matter makes up about 25 percent. The rest is dark energy, which is also a mystery."

---

[1] Jon M. Chang, "'God Particle': Higgs Boson One Year Later," ABC News, July 4, 2013. See http://abcnews.go.com/Technology/god-particle-higgs-boson-year/story?id=19574423 .

[2] Amber Hunt, "Searching For Dark Matter," *Kansas City Star*, November 23, 2012, A2. See also Amber Hunt, "Dark Matter Detector Nearing Activation in SD Mine," Associated Press, November 20, 2012. Accessible at http://bigstory.ap.org/article/dark-matter-detector-nearing-activation-sd-mine .

What? Unlike regular matter and antimatter? I don't know about you, but I'm already two steps behind. I must have slept through that in Physics. To me, this already sounds like science fiction. By my calculation, if regular matter is 4 percent of the universe's mass and dark matter is 25 percent of the universe's mass, then dark energy is 71 percent of the universe's mass, making the unknown universe 96 percent of the total universe. Talk about inspiring confidence. The latter two categories--dark matter and dark energy--make up 96 percent of the mass of the universe? So everything we know is a subset of regular matter (and antimatter), which means that everything we know is a subset of 4 percent of the universe.

And we seem to know very little about that 4 percent.

For example, why do people still use credit cards? Smoke cigarettes? Believe in love? Read books? Kill each other in the name of their gods? There's a lot of mystery right there in the known 4 percent of the universe, not to mention that 96 percent of the universe that we simply infer exists.

Having said all this leads me to conclude that we don't know much, relative to everything there is to know, but that doesn't keep us from our endless quest, as Homo sapiens seem to thrive on the Pyrrhic victory. Or is the Pyrrhic victory the best we can hope for, given the 7.1 billion souls that now inhabit the globe? If we have time to turn things around, if we have time to save ourselves and our planet--with all its wonder and beauty--if we can still find a way to live on the only home we know, may this book bear even a glimmer of light toward this end.

And may we all find a way to learn more and at the same time utilize what we know in the path of peace. For the crisis of our age is not primarily a crisis of knowledge, but a crisis of connectedness, a crisis of community, a crisis of empathy. Empathy is a necessary precondition for even the possibility of community, and global community is a necessary precondition for our very survival as a species. It is possible that empathy cannot be taught, but it can be shown, and perhaps the showing of empathy is the highest form of leadership. It is my hope that it is to this form of leadership that we all aspire.

Somewhere in the Ozark Mountains, July 20, 2013

CHAPTER ONE

HUMAN RIGHTS, DEMOCRACY, AND GLOBAL RENAISSANCE

A

What happened to the American experiment in democracy? Or, as Gore Vidal has maintained, is democracy the last thing our founding fathers intended, since all women, blacks, American Indians, and landless white men were excluded from the democratic voting process––conservatively, over 85% of those living here in the new world?[3]

---

[3] Gore Vidal, interviews with Lila Azam Zanganeh, August 2005 and April 2006, published on August 12, 2013 at www.guernicamag.com/interviews/the-end-of-gore-vidal/ . One short example: "Democracy is something America has never practiced. Because the Founding Fathers hated two things: monarchy and democracy."

Based upon the evidence, one could forcefully argue that those who set up the republic had no intention of allowing real self-governance, but this argument has been made and would require another book altogether. Suffice it to say that, for the purposes of this work, human rights coupled with a democratic process[4] is a societal ordering that is assumed by this writer to be categorically good, by which I mean: something worthy of establishment, something that is, however unrealizable, an ideal to be sought and implemented to the best of our ability at all times and places--something that, in the end, shouldn't be contained within the borders of one nation alone, but must--as a moral imperative--be the model for global political organization.[5] For once human rights are bartered away, everything is negotiable. And once everything is negotiable, personhood as such ceases to exist, replaced by the concept of personhood--the simulacrum that excuses a thousand indiscretions, a thousand body bags, a thousand mass graves.[6]

---

[4] Cf. John Stuart Mill, *On Liberty* (Mineola, NY: Dover Publications, 2002). Originally published in 1859, this work, like many of the works cited in the book, may also be found in the public domain and is available for no charge as an electronic book at www.gutenberg.org (www.gutenberg.org/ebooks/34901). Mill's libertarian argument against the "tyranny of the majority" (a possible outcome of democratic rule) demonstrates why a democracy must be coupled with human rights (often instantiated in some form of a constitution or bill of rights), since without enforceable rights, all subgroups would exist precariously only according to the mercurial vicissitudes of the majority. Today, rather than the tyranny of the majority, we see the "tyranny of the minority"—a slice of the population (perhaps as small as 0.1%) having an overwhelming amount of wealth and influence and therefore seemingly inexorable power. The level of intractability vis à vis the current state of affairs remains to be seen.

It has become evident that our leaders have lost their way, clearly adrift in a sea of Orwellian doublespeak, doublethink and crimestop.[7] They are more than exemplars of the duplicitous princes described 500 years ago by Machiavelli in *The Prince*[8] --for such princes calculated carefully that which would be to their advantage and acted accordingly-- spinning propaganda to serve this end.[9]

---

[5] Certainly, the notion of rights is something that, like all concepts, is in flux and is therefore constantly evolving (or devolving). Given this fact, the discussion and implementation of rights requires constant vigilance, lest the real thing be replaced with an empty shell, a place-holder, a simulacrum. For example, Attorney General Eric Holder's recent pronouncement that the legal right to due process does not necessarily entail (1) the right to have one's day in court and be judged by a jury of one's peers, or (2) the right of habeas corpus, or (3) the right to legal counsel. According to Attorney General Holder, an American citizen can be killed by a Predator drone without having his or her right to due process violated. Thus, in this example we can clearly see that not only the name but the content of rights must be constantly and forcefully reasserted in order to ward off their cooptation, evisceration, and destruction by the corporate-military-industrial complex—all in the name of upholding such rights. See Conor Friedersdorf, "Eric Holder Explains When Drones Can Kill Americans Abroad", *The Atlantic*, March 8, 2012 at www.theatlantic.com/politics/archive/2012/03/eric-holder-explains-when-drones-can-kill-americans-abroad/254168 .

See also John Yoo, "Holder, Drones, and Due Process", *The National Review*, March 6, 2013 at www.nationalreview.com/corner/342335/holder-drones-and-due-process-john-yoo .

See also Josh Gerstein, September 7, 2012 at www.politico.com/blogs/under-the-radar/2012/09/obama-us-seeks-due-process-in-drone-strikes-134889.html . Finally, see Jack Mirkinson, "Jeremy Scahill: Eric Holder's Drone Admission Raises More Questions Than It Answers" (Interview) at www.huffingtonpost.com/2013/05/23/jeremy-scahill-democracy-now-drones_n_3326653.html .

On the nature and extent of the secret drone program in Pakistan alone, see the 182 page report issued in 2012 by the International Human Rights and Conflict Resolution Clinic at Stanford Law School and Global Justice Clinic at NYU School of Law: *Living Under Drones: Death, Injury, and Trauma to Civilians From US Drone Practices in Pakistan* at www.livingunderdrones.org. The first two sentences of the Executive Summary and Recommendations reads: "In the United States, the dominant narrative about the use of drones in Pakistan is of a surgically precise and effective tool that makes the US safer by enabling 'targeted killing' of terrorists, with minimal downsides or collateral impacts. This narrative is false." (v).

But the princes of today are different.[10]   Leaders no longer act even in their own enlightened rational self-interest.[11]   For if they did, they would not make haste to choke the planet to death while stockpiling weapons that could do the job even more quickly, if need be.   Today's leaders exhibit nothing of what may quaintly be described as "rationality"––even in the Machiavellian sense, let alone in the Greek sense of "rationality as prudence" (within a context of virtue) found in, for example, Aristotle's *Nicomachean Ethics*.[12]   The rampant irrationality, stupidity, and banality of today's leaders exhibits more than simply lack of vision, foresight, and imagination (although it certainly does do this), but, following Aristotle, it palpably expresses a lack of character, moral virtue,

---

Finally, for a more comprehensive account of the administration's drone program, see Medea Benjamin, *Drone Warfare: Killing By Remote Control* (New York: Verso, 2013).   This is the updated edition of the OR book, originally published in 2012. Regarding the use of drones, Benjamin writes: "So a principle of innocent until proven guilty has morphed into a policy of guilty, and dead, until proven innocent. (And even this possibility of a posthumous declaration of innocence is a cruel joke, since the US makes little effort to identify all those killed or injured, much less investigate their backgrounds.)" (8).

[6] The loss of due process, even for Americans, is no longer theoretical. It is now a matter of general knowledge.   Even *USA Today* notes, regarding Obama's drone program, that "the victims, the administration acknowledged Wednesday [May 22, 2013], have included four U.S. citizens..." *USA Today*, Friday, May 24, 2013, 12A. Attorney General Eric Holder's Orwellian due process at work.   Michael Shank, director of foreign policy at the Friends Committee on National Legislation, notes in the same issue of *USA Today* that "We are disposing of past precedent [when killing with drones] and throwing conventions to the curb with our willingness to kill Americans outside the court of law with little prosecutorial evidence, our secret White House kill list, and our erroneous belief that strikes are strategic." See *USA Today*, Friday, May 24, 2013, 12A.

On the "secret" Presidential meetings on "Terror Tuesdays" to discuss candidates for the White House kill list, see Jo Becker and Scott Shane, "Secret 'kill list' Proves a Test of Obama's Principles and Will," *New York Times*, May 29, 2012.   See http://www.nytimes.com/2012/05/29/world/obamas-leadership-in-war-on-al-qaeda.html?pagewanted=all&_r=0 .

and goodness.[13]

---

[7] See George Orwell, *1984* (New York: Harcourt Brace and Company, 2003). Originally published in 1949. See in particular the Appendix: The Principles of Newspeak, 309-323, for strikingly evident parallels to the present world situation. For example, warrantless surveillance under the apparent auspices of The Patriot Act, Section 215, distorted to include dragnet surveillance of "280 million Americans", with the collection of hundreds or thousands of records per American (According to William Binney, 40 year National Security Agency veteran and whistleblower). Binney stated on June 6, 2013 that "Probably three billion phone records on Americans have been collected every day" since September 11, 2001— and this is not including email communications. Recently, based upon the leak from former NSA contractor and former CIA employee Edward Snowden to Glenn Greenwald at *The Guardian*, we have found that the FBI had issued a secret subpoena to Verizon (even Verizon is forbidden to disclose the existence of the subpoena), ordering Verizon to release tens of millions of phone records; purportedly, every single one of their phone records is covered. See Nick Hopkins, "UK Gathering Secret Intelligence via Covert NSA Operation," *The Guardian,* June 7, 2013 at http://www.guardian.co.uk/technology/2013/jun/07/uk-gathering-secret-intelligence-nsa-prism?guni=Network%20front:network-front%20full-width-1%20bento-box:Bento%20box:Position3 .

Thomas Drake (also a whistleblower from the National Security Agency) stated that the leak merely represents what goes on every single day, and that the secret collection of data on tens of millions of Americans is simply business as usual. See *Democracy Now* interview with William Binney, Thomas Drake and Shayana Kadidal   at http://www.democracynow.org/2013/6/6/nsa_whistleblowers_all_us_citizens_targeted . The data collection goes far beyond the mere collection of tens of millions of phone records. In fact, if you are reading this, it seems eminently reasonable to conclude that your phone and electronic communications have been collected and stored, and this is only based upon a small glimpse of the covert programs.

Additionally, see interviews by Amy Goodman at *Democracy Now* with Edward Snowden ("Even if you're not doing anything wrong, you're being watched and recorded."), Glenn Greenwald and William Binney ("The government is not trying to protect [secrets about NSA surveillance] from the terrorists. It's trying to protect knowledge of that program from the citizens of the United States.") at http://www.democracynow.org/shows/2013/6/10 .

What we are dealing with is that single thing with which the post-Moderns have had so much trouble: moral evil.[14] Sure you can, at this juncture, attack the messenger.[15] Now's the time to do that. But, unfortunately, I am not some kind of conspiracy theorist or cult member, nor am I on some kind of hallucinogenic drug trip (although sometimes it feels like it when I survey the state of our planet). On the contrary, I am an American philosopher, and I've been a philosopher for thirty years––trained at multiple American universities––and I have taught philosophy at American colleges and universities for twenty-seven years. What I have observed in the leadership in this country––and among the global elite (a large subset of which are one and the same) over the last thirty years

---

The administration's response has been swift and obfuscational in coming: "The programs 'make a difference in our capacity to anticipate and prevent possible terrorist activity,' Obama said." See Peter Finn and Ellen Nakashima, "Obama Defends Sweeping Surveillance Program," *The Washington Post,* June 7, 2013 at http://www.washingtonpost.com/blogs/post-politics/wp/2013/06/07/obama-nobody-is-listening-to-your-telephone-calls/ : "The Washington Post reported Friday that the National Security Agency and the FBI are tapping directly into the central servers of nine leading U.S. Internet companies, extracting audio and video chats, photographs, e-mails, documents, and connection logs that enable analysts to track foreign targets." The government "evidence" (if they deign to say they have any. Such "evidence", would, of course, remain classified) for such flagrant and ongoing violations of the rights of United States citizens is based upon "secret laws" and the secret interpretation of laws. Secret laws? Secret interpretations? What could be more Kafkaesque? How about a secret speed limit? Or a secret right to vote? Or a secret election result? How about a secret diploma when you graduate from the university? Why not simply imprison everyone in order to reduce the crime rate? With everyone in solitary confinement, violent crime would be sure to drop. Terrorism would be zero. Sounds like a win-win situation. Welcome to post-rational Orwellian Newspeak. But maybe Newspeak is in fact Oldspeak: Cf. Thucydides, *History of the Peloponnesian War,* ed. M. I. Finley and trans. Rex Warner (New York: Penguin, 1972) and Myra MacPherson, *"All Governments Lie": The Life and Times of Rebel Journalist I. F. Stone"* (New York: Scribner, 2008).

Finally, see Glenn Greenwald interview: "Rogue" Actions of U.S. in Snowden Row Yield Latin American Offers of Asylum, *Democracy Now,* July 8, 2013. Accessible at http://www.democracynow.org/2013/7/8/glenn_greenwald_rogue_actions_of_us .

has been nothing less than appalling. The clear moral bankruptcy, the preying upon the weak, the helpless, the homeless, the poor, the destitute, the hungry, the disenfranchised[16]--has been nothing less than the machinations of the morally insane, the sociopathic.[17] For sociopathy, as a moral category, is within the domain of the moral philosopher, not the social scientist--and as a philosopher I pronounce judgment: in a time of copious plenty, those who would strive to

---

[8]Niccolò Machiavelli, *The Prince*, trans. N.H. Thomson (Mineola, NY: Dover Publications, 1992). Originally published in 1513, this short work is a searing, horrifying and illuminating treatise on realpolitik. Machiavelli notes that in order to gain, maintain and consolidate power, one must give up all ideals save power itself (which could be viewed as an inverse ideal). All forms of machination and dissembling are fair game in the pursuit of this "ideal", as one must always be something other than what one appears to be. For Machiavelli, cognition and affection must always serve an enlightened self-interest. In this sense, contemporary leaders are post-Machiavellian, since even enlightened self-interest has been jettisoned. Note that Machiavelli wasn't advocating such realpolitik, he was merely describing what one must expect to do in order to acquire and maintain power.

[9] The extent to which the multinational media-industrial complex currently controls access to information and therefore public opinion and worldview is a matter of debate. The debate concerns only the degree to which this is the case, not the existence of such control. Clearly, such power is a means by which the democratic process and human rights can be (and are) subverted.

[10] If human nature remains constant, one might argue that the situation today cannot be fundamentally different (worse) than that found in any other epoch. This will be addressed as we proceed. But even if the premise is granted (that human nature is a constant), this does not settle the issue, for the means to perpetrate evil upon one's neighbors have become exponentially more powerful and at the same time much more accessible. Now, as we are all abundantly aware, a small group could cause the death of millions. Cf. Carl Jung, *The Undiscovered Self, trans. R.F.C. Hull* (New York: Mentor, 1958). Welcome to the age of unmitigated universal terror.

[11] If this claim is correct, we may already be living in a post-human world, a world created by those who feign humanity.

[12] Aristotle, *Nicomachean Ethics*, 2nd edition, trans. Terence Irwin (Indianapolis: Hackett Publishing Company, 1999). Aristotle lived in the fourth century BCE. Aristotle espoused what now seems to be the quaint notion that reason, that unique capacity we have as human beings, could and should be used to develop our virtues and that the development of character was a lifelong process of concerted reason and will.

deprive the poor of even that which they need to live are morally insane, morally evil. Those who act in such a manner are therefore without excuse, and their behavior, the behavior of the morally insane, is reprehensible (but clearly, not to them).[18]

---

[13] It is at this juncture that I wish to make an important distinction that will serve to illuminate the discussion throughout the course of this work, and that is the distinction between **descriptive** and **normative** claims. The standard explanation is that scientists, be they natural scientists (biology, chemistry, etc.) or social scientists (anthropology, sociology, psychology, economics) describe the world as it is, that is: they tell us what is the case, what the facts are. But scientific methodology, in telling us what *is* the case, doesn't tell us what *ought to be* the case. A normative claim is a claim about what ought to be the case: it goes beyond the expression of facts, to the realm of value, derived from the summation of facts. It is a judgment concerning right and wrong. It is the injection of the moral universe into the empirical universe. It is what gives meaning to "reality". The descriptive is the realm of the scientist. For example: asking an economist—a social scientist— to tell us what actions we ought (normative) to take when it comes to the economy is asking the economist to operate outside of his or her (descriptive) field. The economist is perfectly justified in stating "If we do X, then A will happen, or if we do Y, then B will happen (even if they are often wrong), because they are prognosticating based upon the data, not making policy decisions based upon normative assumptions. Conclusion: allowing Federal Reserve Chairman Ben Bernanke, an economist, to make normative policy decisions (Quantitative Easing 1, 2, 3…ad infinitum) is like asking a professional baseball player to compete in the Indy 500. Hey, it could work out, but the odds are against it—and if there's a crash, a whole lot of people could go down. The normative is about value. It is about passion, intuition and imagination. It goes beyond mere description, calculation and quantification. The normative is the realm of the artist, the musician, the writer, the philosopher. Philosophy without expression of value is in itself empty of value.

[14] Given such an assertion—that real (and possibly intractable) moral evil exists— we must dispense with utopian notions for social organization and operate based upon the exigencies of human behavior. To begin, we must dispense with any hope for a classless, egalitarian society and (what may be one and the same, or at least exhibits significant overlap) we must dispense with the notion of the possibility of the abolition of government. Given these parameters, we must not become despondent but continue to seek distributive justice and human rights. Put differently: there will always be social and economic stratification and there will always be some form of government (even if they are essentially multinational cartels), but this does not mean we should not work for social, political and economic justice. Rather, such parameters provide a clear impetus to engage in the process of the promotion of democracy and human rights.

In making such a claim, I argue that persuasion is no longer possible: rationality has been turned on its head and itself made an instrument of terror; language has been perverted into an instrument of deception––and truth, to those in control––is anathema. Truth has been replaced by its simulacrum––"truth". Facts, as such, no longer exist in a world of endless spin; objective reality has been replaced by subjective opinion treated as objective

---

[15] Attacking the messenger has become and ever-increasing part of the standard state apparatus for maintaining secrecy regarding the violations of human rights, both at home and abroad. Note, for example the governmental responses to whistleblowing NSA employees William Binney and Thomas Drake (It remains to be seen what will happen to Edward Snowden). Concerning Bradley Manning, arrested May 2010 (and finally now on trial) see www.gurdian.co.uk/world/bradley-manning , www.democracynow.org/topics/bradley-manning , http://topics.nytimes.com/top/reference/timestopics/people/m/bradley_e man ning/index.html , Kevin Goszlula, "Bradley Manning's trial, NSA Leaks and the Ever-Increasing Secrecy of the National Security State" June 9, 2013 at http://firedoglake.com/bradley-manning-coverage/ . Finally, you may access the official Facebook page of the Bradley Manning Support Network at www.facebook.com/savebradley or go directly to the Bradley Manning Support Network at www.bradleymanning.org.

Concerning Australian Julian Assange (who has been granted political asylum in Ecuador but is now in the Ecuadorian Embassy in London because he has been denied safe passage to Ecuador) see www.guardian.co.uk/media/julian-assange , www.huffingtonpost.com/news/julian-assange/ , http://topics.nytimes.com/top/reference/timestopics/people/a/julian_p_assan ge/index.html, www.foxnews.com/topics/world/julian-assange.htm , www.democracynow.org/appearances/julian_assange .

reality.[19]

Reality thus becomes merely a matter of taste, a function of point-of-view––and since everyone has a point of view, nothing is ever actually true. Doesn't this sound precisely like a description of mass psychosis, collective delusion, specious groupthink (a function of the leadership of the morally insane)? Is there any real thinking going on? Other than as a means to create new spin, that is? Certainly, denial of objective reality is a way to jettison any semblance of a moral universe, and, by extension, to erase any ground for real moral accountability.

---

[16] One clear example in this regard is the ongoing societal disenfranchisement vis à vis higher education (as well as K-12 education). More and more desperate students shell out more and more money for an education that provides less and less. See Joseph E. Stiglitz, "Student Debt and the Crushing of the American Dream," *New York Times,* May 12, 2013. Accessible at http://opinionator.blogs.nytimes.com/2013/05/12/student-debt-and-the-crushing-of-the-american-dream/ . Stiglitz writes, "America is distinctive among advanced industrialized countries in the burden it places on students and their parents for financing higher education. America is also exceptional among comparable countries for the high cost of a college degree, including public universities...we are foreclosing on our future as a nation...As has been repeatedly observed, *all* of the economic gains since the Great Recession [2008-2009] have gone to the top 1%...Robust higher education, with healthy public support, was once the linchpin in a system that promised opportunity for dedicated students of any means. We now have a pay-to-play, winner-take-all game where the wealthiest are assured a spot, and the rest are compelled to take a gamble on huge debts, with no guarantee of a payoff."

See Also Greg Kaufmann, "This Week in Poverty: Taking On Sallie Mae and the Cost of Education," *The Nation,* May 31, 2013. Accessible at http://www.thenation.com/blog/174597/week-poverty-taking-sallie-mae-and-cost-education# . Kaufmann writes, "The promise of privatization of the student loan industry was that there would be greater efficiency and therefore more opportunities for students to pay for college and thrive. This is clearly not what Sallie Mae and the big banks have delivered to students..." Now, 38.8 million Americans have student loans, totaling over $1,100,000,000,000 (yes, that's 1.1 trillion dollars, and climbing—more than all credit card debt combined), and 31% of those in the repayment phase are "seriously delinquent" (or have defaulted) on their payments.

Certainly, the leaders of a failed planet would want to do this. But why would we--as subjects of the failed sociopathic plan-- want to do this? It has now become clear that the subjects of this failed sociopathic plan we call the global economy no longer wish to be subject to such a plan, nor to its revisions in their multifarious forms: austerity, quantitative easing, budget-slashing--and the suppression, infringement and destruction of myriad rights (freedom of

---

As of July 1, 2013, federal student loan rates have doubled: See Stephan Dinan, "Democrats Defy Obama and the Republicans as Student Loan Rates Double," *Washington Times,* July 8, 2013. Dinan writes, "Student loan rates rose July 1 after Congress failed to agree on a solution to keep them at the 3.4 percent rate enacted in 2010." It remains to be seen whether Congress will retroactively reduce the rate to the previous 3.4%, return rates to 3.4% in the future, or do nothing. Some, including President Obama, have suggested that we tie the rate of the student loans to the rate of the Treasury's 10-year note—which would effectively eliminate fixed-rate federal student loans, turning them into adjustable rate financial products. This is just one more clear example of those in charge being incapable of coming up with any good ideas when it comes to being fair to people who actually have to work for a living. See article at http://www.washingtontimes.com/news/2013/jul/8/democrats-defy-obama-and-republicans-as-student-lo/?page=all .

[17] I use the term in its technical sense. See Martha Stout, *The Sociopath Next Door* (New York: Broadway Books, 2005). Dr. Stout writes, "Many mental health professionals refer to the condition of little or no conscience as 'antisocial personality disorder,' a noncorrectable disfigurement of character that is now thought to be present in about 4 percent of the population—that is to say, one in twenty-five people. This condition of missing conscience is called by other names, too, most often 'sociopathy,' or the somewhat more familiar term *psychopathy.* Guiltlessness was in fact the first personality disorder to be recognized by psychiatry, and terms that have been used at times over the past century include *manie sans délire, psychopathic inferiority, moral insanity, and moral imbecility."* *(6).*

For seminal research on psychopathy/sociopathy, see Robert D. Hare, *Without Conscience: The Disturbing World of the Psychopaths Among Us* (New York: The Guilford Press, 1999).

Additional neuroscience on the issue can be found in James Blair, Derek Mitchell and Karina Blair, *The Psychopath: Emotion and the Brain* (Malden, MA: Blackwell Publishing, 2005).

See also Robert D. Hare, *The Psychopathy Checklist – Revised, 2nd Edition* (Toronto: Multi-Health Systems, 2003).

assembly, speech, the press, habeas corpus, among others. More about this in part B of this essay).[20]

The transcendent wail of liberation is now boundless.

In 2011 alone, there were reportable and reported protests, demonstrations, uprisings, riots and civil wars in at least 82 countries, among them: Antarctica, Argentina, Australia, Austria, Bahrain, Bangladesh, Belgium, Bosnia, Brazil, Bulgaria, Canada, Chile, Colombia, Costa Rica, Croatia, Czech Republic, Denmark, Dominican Republic, England, Ecuador, Egypt, Estonia, Finland, France, Germany, Greece, Hungary, Iceland, India, Iran, Ireland, Israel, Italy, Japan, Kosovo, Macedonia, Malaysia, Mexico, Montenegro, the Netherlands,

---

[18] The empirical description of sociopathy we do well to leave to science (see preceding note). As a philosopher interested in social, economic and political justice, I would argue that the citizens of any given society would not be well served by having sociopaths in positions of power—in either the public or private sectors. Once this point is conceded, we are in a position to begin to discuss possible societal restructurings with a view to blocking the ongoing implementation of structures of systemic sociopathy.

[19] Once everything is effectively treated as subjective, i.e., as a matter of opinion, as a matter of perspective, as a function of one's situation in the world (rich, poor, black, brown, male, female), all truth claims, as such, become unintelligible. Moral epistemology is a subset of epistemology proper. If truth is no longer possible, moral truth is no longer possible. If moral truth is no longer possible, sociopathy is no longer a pathological condition. If sociopathy is no longer a pathological condition, what becomes of humanity qua humanity?

[20] At this juncture it would be wise to look at two documents: (1) *The United States Constitution*, with special attention to Amendments 1 – 10 (collectively referred to as the *Bill of Rights*), accessible at http://constitutionus.com/ and (2) *The United Nations Universal Declaration of Human Rights*, ratified by the United Nations General Assembly on December 10, 1948, accessible at www.un.org/en/documents/udhr . See part B of this essay for more specifics on human rights.

New Zealand, Nicaragua, Norway, Palestine (West Bank and Gaza Strip), Peru, Poland, Portugal, Puerto Rico, Pakistan, Romania, Serbia, Singapore, Slovakia, Slovenia, South Korea, Spain, Sweden, Switzerland, Syria, Taiwan, Tunisia, and the United States.[21] As I write this in June 2013, there are ongoing uprisings in Syria, Cyprus, China, Russia, Cambodia, Pakistan, Ethiopia, Palestine, Iraq, Afghanistan, Turkey, Egypt, Brazil and Japan. How many have died? How many have been injured?

Paralleling the universality of the protests is the uncanny universality of governmental responses to such protests, responses that consist of overwhelming force and violence. This is the case regardless of stated governmental form--republic, democracy, communistic-centralized economy, laissez faire, theocratic dictatorship, secular dictatorship. Regardless of overt governmental form or degree of centralization or decentralization, when the elite class is challenged, it responds with threats, terror, and blunt force--even given the fact that the vast majority of the protests have been peaceful, comprised of students, professionals, small business owners, senior citizens, and members of the police and armed forces.

---

[21] See Simon Rogers, Monday, 14 November 2011 at www.guardian.uk/news/datablog/2011/oct/17/occupy-protests-world-list-map for more detail and a breakdown on the protests occurring on every continent. People of every religion, race, and creed are standing up to what they perceive as a rigged system where a very small segment of the world's population owns and controls an overwhelming proportion of the world's resources, effectively relegating the remaining majority to a life of poverty, violence, sickness, suffering, or death.

The protesters are met with tear gas and tear gas canisters (sometimes lethal), weapons grade pepper spray, tanks, heavy equipment, and police in riot gear with helmets and faceshields wielding truncheons and shooting rubber bullets (and sometimes real bullets) as governments attempt to quell (unsuccessfully) through terror the ever-increasing global tide of unrest.

The only basis for the possibility of change is on the grounds of a true renaissance of awareness. Such a renaissance will entail both cognitive and affective (read: moral) components, for without a moral impetus, without a moral compass, without a cry for justice, without ethical parameters, renaissance cannot begin nor take shape in any meaningful way.[22] This is what we shall call the hermeneutic of freedom, the hermeneutic of liberation, the hermeneutic of enlightenment, the hermeneutic of resistance, for in the end, each requires the other, and they are all a function of collective being-in-the-world.

French-Algerian philosopher and writer Albert Camus wrote a fascinating, trenchant and seemingly forgotten work (appearing in 1951 in French), titled *The Rebel: An Essay on Man in Revolt*.[23] In this work, Camus details what he refers to as the history of "metaphysical rebellion": that point of perceived injustice beyond which humanity will not passively suffer, that point beyond which humanity will rebel in order to secure for itself a more just and equitable manner of living (or merely for the ability to live at all).

---

[22] Everything tends toward chaos, but not oblivion.

[23] Albert Camus, *The Rebel: An Essay on Man in Revolt,* trans. Anthony Bower (New York : Vintage, 1956).

Simply put, if people are treated badly enough and for long enough, they will revolt to set things right--even if the odds are a long shot and they risk imminent death. Camus argues--as a philosopher is wont to do--that the precipitating factors in the rebellion are not a function of culture (although they will invariably be culturally conditioned) but are in fact derived from a transcultural and transhistorical moral sense--a sense of justice and injustice, right and wrong, good and evil.[24] Such a transcultural and transhistorical moral sense is the necessary and sufficient condition for the possibility of renaissance, a renaissance which will, in turn, allow for the possibility of meaningful and directed social and political action--praxis in the concrete world in which we have been thrown and within which we are forced to make choices, sometimes choices of life and death. And if we are by circumstance forced to make such choices, why not make them with a view toward the light? Why not make them thinking of the next generation, or the one beyond that? With a renaissance of cognitive and affective awareness, such choice can move from the realm of dream to the realm of vision to the realm of plan to the realm of execution. Consequently, a renaissance of cognitive and affective awareness provides grounds for hope based on concrete material conditions rather than upon some ethereal *deus ex machina*. For it is undoubtedly the case that not all hope is created equal. Hope generated through a renaissance of cognitive and affective awareness is a

---

[24] It goes without saying that the sociopath, based upon the preceding discussion, would not experience such a renaissance. Clearly, anything that goes without saying is inherently problematic for the philosopher, so I am saying it here. The underlying axiom, of course, is that we should carefully uncover and assess our assumptions (premises). Of course, even the axiom itself can be questioned.

universal hope for all peoples the world over, a hope rooted in universal co-participation: a universal praxis of hope. Transcending all cognitive constructs[25] and therefore all sectarian orthodoxies, such a renaissance of cognitive and affective awareness provides concrete hope and a vision for our collective, global life together. The tools are not a matter of technology or technique. They are, rather, found within and available to all who seek them.

If the aim of the empathete (one who, through empathy, identifies with all living things) is to live within the cognitive and affective light of the renaissance, a corollary, an epiphenomenon, if you will, of such awareness will be to lead--as a Sherpa guide--others who are on a similar journey. The Sherpa, even as leader, does not walk for the other. The Sherpa walks along with the other, as they both seek the same destination.

The evidence for the possibility of such a renaissance of awareness and the attendant hermeneutic of freedom/liberation/enlightenment/resistance is an inductive one, based upon the contingencies and exigencies of history. We have provided a glimpse of such evidence in the form of resistance--the protests within scores of nation-states that comprise over half of the world's living human inhabitants.

---

[25] That is, the basis of renaissance, involving both cognitive and affective components, necessarily exceeds the limits of cognition alone. Given this, the basis of renaissance can never be thoroughly adumbrated and therefore cannot be the object of understanding (thus any calculative model will fail to comprehend human behavior). Existential and phenomenological analysis grants limited access to the limitless nature of the experience of renaissance.

And for the hard-headed empiricist, the radical skeptic, this evidence is necessary but possibly insufficient--as can be said of all evidence presented to a finite, fallible, subjective being on a small planet spinning and hurtling through space.[26] This is where the objective way breaks off, but yet truth remains-- the truth of our own lived experience.[27]

In acknowledging the validity of our own experience we allow for the possibility of a renaissance of cognitive and affective awareness, a renaissance that taps into heirloom seed long buried but dormant until tilled and watered and nurtured with hope for the future. It is this seed that the monolithic global corporate-totalitarian machine seeks to extinguish forever, as it prepares the ground for the arrival of the post-human world. It is, therefore, our very humanity that we assert as we stand against the

---

[26] Cf. David Hume, *Treatise of Human Nature*, ed. T.H. Green and T.H. Grose (London: Longmans, Green, and Co., 1886) and David Hume, *An Enquiry Concerning Human Understanding* (Mineola, NY: Dover Publications, 2004). Hume (1711-1776) was a Scottish philosopher famous for his radically skeptical empiricism. He maintained, essentially, that all we as humans could really know were our perceptions, not the things in themselves (and, of course, there may be no such "things in themselves").   Put differently, we can't escape our own "subjectivity" to actually get to the "objective" world, so what we call "knowledge" is in fact conceptualized sense impression and nothing more. Even if this is the case, the empathete may utilize his/her cognitive and affective awareness to move forward with the hermeneutic of freedom, liberation, enlightenment and resistance—for if one's own lived experience is not grounds for acting in this world, there can be no such grounds.

[27] Cf. Søren Kierkegaard, *The Concluding Unscientific Postscript to the Philosophical Fragments*, trans. David F. Swenson and Walter Lowrie (Princeton, NJ: Princeton University Press, 1968). Kierkegaard (1813-1855) is often called the father of modern existentialism. This work, which appeared in Danish in 1846, was written under the philosophical pseudonym Johannes Climacus and expresses much of the skepticism of rationality found in Hume. Kierkegaard refused to sign his own name to any of his many philosophical works (utilizing instead a number of pseudonyms. He did, however, sign his religious works), further expressing, one may argue, his skepticism of inductive and deductive truth, and, indeed, "knowledge" itself.

erasure of our own freedom, liberation and enlightenment. Once these are gone, this essay will no longer make sense. Now, in this, the only time in which we are living, we struggle to resist those who would disarm us.

B

Now we shall look at (1) The *United States Constitution*[28] and (2) The *Universal Declaration of Human Rights*[29], with a view toward noting some of the more flagrant and egregious civil and human rights violations.[30]

---

[28] Accessible at http://constitutionus.com/

[29] Accessible at www.un.org/en/documents/udhr .

[30] "Civil rights", as I am using the term here, refers to rights enumerated by the *United States Constitution*. "Human rights" refers to rights enumerated by the General Assembly of the United Nations in the *Universal Declaration of Human Rights*. Civil rights and human rights, of course, are not mutually exclusive. On the contrary, the former, ideally, should be drawn from the latter. The meta-political source of human rights, if such exists, is not a subject of this work. That is to say, I leave the question concerning the ultimate origin or source of human rights to the reader. The argument I present in this work does not require one to accept that human rights are of metaphysical origin (metaphysical origin = God or gods, or natural or moral law somehow instantiated in the universe—rather than merely being something invented by humanity and promulgated and enforced by nation-states), nor does it require one to deny that human rights are of metaphysical origin. It requires only that one recognize the existence or potential existence of rights agreed upon and enforced by national or transnational actors. In this way, we avoid getting sidetracked by the thorny metaphysical issues and proffered proofs that may have importance and interest for some, but are in no way essential to moving forward in the real world with issues related to civil and human rights. Theory may have its own allure, but what we are interested in are coherent and enforceable civil and human rights.

We shall begin with the *United States Constitution* (1787), in particular, Amendments 1 – 10, collectively known as the *Bill of Rights* (1791). Those enumerated in abbreviated form are those that have been infringed, truncated, or otherwise violated.[31] I have enumerated the specific rights within each amendment. Your numbering may be different. Follow the footnotes in part A of this chapter in addition to the other essays in this book to get a fuller

---

[31] For a start, see "Is Edward Snowden a Hero? A Debate with Journalist Chris Hedges & Law Scholar Geoffrey Stone", *Democracy Now*, June 12, 2013 at http://www.democracynow.org/2013/6/12/is_edward_snowden_a_hero_a .
Chris Hedges: "Well, we're talking about the death of a free press, the death of a civil society. This is far beyond a reasonable debate. We make the East German Stasi state look like the Boy Scouts. And if we don't wrest back this power for privacy, for the capacity to investigate what our power elite is doing, I think we can essentially say our democracy has been snuffed out."
See also: "Chris Hedges: Monitoring of AP Phones a "Terrifying" Step in State Assault on Press Freedom", *Democracy Now* interview with Amy Goodman and Nermeen Shaikh, May 15, 2013 at http://www.democracynow.org/2013/5/15/chris_hedges_monitoring_of_ap_phones .
Amy Goodman: "Your response to this revelation about the—about what happened with AP and the U.S. government?"
Chris Hedges: "Well, it's part of a pattern. That's what's so frightening. And it's a pattern that we've seen, with the use of the Espionage Act, to essentially silence whistleblowers within the government—Kiriakou, Drake and others, although Kiriakou went to jail on—pled out on another charge—the FISA Amendment Act, which allows for warrantless wiretapping, the National Defense Authorization Act, which allows for the stripping of American citizens of due process and indefinite detention. And it is one more assault in a long series of assaults against freedom of information and freedom of the press. And I would also, of course, throw in the persecution of Julian Assange at WikiLeaks and Bradley Manning as part of that process."
Nermeen Shaikh: "Well, Chris Hedges, you wrote in the recent article that was published, your article "Death of Truth" in Truthdig [www.truthdig.com
] and [The] *Nation* magazine— you also write about the significance of the Espionage Act and how often it's been invoked, and you say that it eviscerates the possibility of an independent press. So could you talk about the Espionage Act and how it also is somehow related to this AP story?"

picture of the nature and extent of civil and human rights violations. As always, don't take my word for it. Draw your own conclusions from the full body of each text.[32]

PART ONE: CIVIL RIGHTS
THE *UNITED STATES CONSTITUTION* (IN PART): THE *BILL OF RIGHTS*, Amendments 1 – 10, omitting Amendments 3 and 7:

Chris Hedges: "Well, it's been used six times by the Obama administration. It was written in 1917 and was—is our Foreign Secrets Act. It is never meant—it was not designed to shut down whistleblowers, first used against Daniel Ellsberg in the Pentagon Papers. So, three times from 1917 until Obama takes office in 2009, six times. And if you talk to investigative journalists in this country, who must investigate the inner workings of government, no one will talk, even on background. People are terrified. And this is, of course—the seizure of two months of records, of AP records, is not really about going after AP; it's about going after that person or those people who leaked this story and shutting them down. And this canard that it endangered American life is—you know, there's no evidence for this."

See also "Michael Moore, Chris Hedges on Challenging NDAA Indefinite Detention and the "Corporate Coup d'État", *Democracy Now* interview, February 11, 2013 at http://www.democracynow.org/2013/2/11/michael_moore_chris_h edges_on_challenging .

See also John W. Whitehead, "Terror Tuesdays, Kill Lists and Drones: Has the President Become a Law Unto Himself?", *The Rutherford Institute*, June 18, 2012, at https://www.rutherford.org/publications_resources/john_whitehe ads_commentary/terror_tuesdays_kill_lists_and_drones_has_the_p resident_become_a_law_unto_h .

See also Dylan Stableford, "Obama's 'secret kill list' shows President is Final Word on Terrorist Killing Missions," ABC news, May 29, 2012, at http://abcnews.go.com/Politics/OTUS/obamas-secret-kill-list-shows-president-final-word/story?id=16449862#.Ubo4s-tifjE .

For extensive information on the kill list and drones, see Raymond T. Pronk, *Pronk Palisades,* May 31, 2012, at http://raymondpronk.wordpress.com/2012/05/31/obamas-kill-list-on-terrorist-tuesdays-obama-targets-innocent-civilian-and-american-terrorists-videos/ .

On assassination of US citizens, see Glenn Greenwald, "Chilling Legal Memo From Obama DOJ Justifies Assassination of US Citizens," *The Guardian*, February 5, 2013, at http://www.guardian.co.uk/commentisfree/2013/feb/05/obama-kill-list-doj-memo .

Amendment 1: (1) Freedom of Speech, (2) of the press, and (3) the right of people to peaceably assemble.

Amendment 2: (4) The right to keep and bear arms.

Amendment 4: (5) Unreasonable search and seizure, (6) probable cause.

Amendment 5: (7) No person shall be…deprived of life, liberty, or property, without due process of law.

Amendment 6: (8) Speedy and public trial, (9) be informed of nature and cause of accusations, (10) to be confronted with witnesses, (11) right to call witnesses, (12) right to counsel.

Amendment 8: (13) Right against cruel and unusual punishment.

Amendment 9: (14) Nonenumerated rights shall be retained by the people.

Amendment 10: (15) State's rights. [This right is the only right I enumerate here that is ostensibly not an individual right, but a collective right of a subgroup over and against the federal government].[33]

See also Michael Boyle, "Obama's Drone Wars and the Normalisation of Extrajudicial Murder," *The Guardian*, June 11, 2012, at http://www.guardian.co.uk/commentisfree/2012/jun/11/obama-drone-wars-normalisation-extrajudicial-killing .
See also Mark Memmott, "A 'Macabre' Process: Nominating Terrorists to Nation's 'Kill List'," *National Public Radio*, May 29, 2012, at http://www.npr.org/blogs/thetwo-way/2012/05/29/153929049/a-macabre-process-nominating-terrorists-to-nations-kill-list .
Finally, see James Bamford, "The Secret War," *Wired,* June 12, 2013. Accessible at http://www.wired.com/threatlevel/2013/06/general-keith-alexander-cyberwar/all/ .

[32] Incoherent or indefensible rights are not rights in theory; theoretical rights that are not defended are not rights in fact. Vigilance, collective action, and sufficient power are required to promulgate and enforce civil and human rights.

[33] Once again, please consult the full text, accessible at http://constitutionus.com/ .

PART TWO: HUMAN RIGHTS

THE *UNIVERSAL DECLARATION OF HUMAN RIGHTS* (1948), SELECTIONS, abbreviated and paraphrased:[34]

Articles 1: All persons are born with rights.

Article 2: No distinction shall be made on the basis of the political, jurisdictional or international status of the country or territory to which a person belongs.

Article 3: Right to life, liberty and security.

Article 4: Right not be held in slavery or servitude.

Article 5: Right against torture and cruel, inhuman or degrading treatment.

Article 8: Right to legal redress if fundamental rights are violated.

Article 9: Right against arbitrary arrest, detention or exile.

Article 10: Right to fair, independent and public hearing when charged with criminal offense.

Article 11: Right to presumption of innocence.

Article 12: Right to privacy.

Article 14: Right to seek asylum from persecution.

Article 18: Right to freedom of thought, conscience and religion.

Article 19: Rights to freedom of speech and of the press.

Article 20: Right to peaceful assembly.

Article 21 (3): "The will of the people [emphasis mine] shall be the basis of the authority of government..."

Article 23: Right to work and protection against unemployment. Right to just remuneration.

Article 24: Right to reasonable limitations on working hours.

---

[34] Once again, please consult the full text, accessible at www.un.org/en/documents/udhr .

Article 25: Right to food, clothing, housing, medical care and social services.
Article 26: Right to an education.
Article 30: Right against the destruction of any rights set forth in the *Universal Declaration of Human Rights*.

QUESTIONS:
 (1) Should human beings have civil rights? If you think so, take a look at the *Bill of Rights*. Are there any civil rights you would eliminate? If so, why? If you do not think that human beings should have civil rights, explain why you think this. Would you employ an alternative concept to talk about individual moral grievances over and against the state?
 (2) Given your knowledge at this time, has the United States (government or corporate actors, or other actors) violated any of your civil rights? Has the United States (government or corporate actors, or other actors) violated the civil rights of anyone other than you, as far as you know? Explain.
 (3) If your answer to question two is yes, what do you think should be done?

CHAPTER TWO

CLASS WARFARE? ARE YOU KIDDING?

Class warfare? Are you kidding? The oppressed against the oppressor? Wouldn't both parties have to know that there is a war going on? Or, is this in fact a case of "liberation" that just looks like a war? What? Haven't we heard that somewhere before? Let's work with the assumption that a war implies that the disputants have been notified prior to the commencement of hostilities. But our situation is quite different, what with overt and covert hostilities–– through act of Congress, Supreme Court edict, Executive branch cabal, corporate malfeasance. No, this isn't precisely a war, since a war implies, if not notification, hostility.

But here, the hostility is one-sided, while victims endlessly endeavor to ingratiate themselves with post-Machiavellians masquerading as benefactors. The deniers are right, they were always right: this isn't class warfare at all. It's more like a slow poisoning. For how can anyone respect someone who swallows wholesale the lies of the liar?

The liar's disrespect for the sycophant morphs to hatred, demanding to be requited. There isn't going to be any tearful breakup. The death elixir is administered to the adoring, trusting gossamer of humanity as they are wiped clean from the earth and from the memory of the earth, vanquished forevermore. Undoubtedly, this is a poisoning, a poisoning of the starry-eyed lover who wants nothing more than to be with the beloved, to serve the beloved, to become the beloved. The trust is unilateral, as is the mendacity. The lover serves in spite of herself, the lover cannot help but trust, since the lover cannot help but love. The lover sees truth, light, goodness, and so is blind to the dissembling, is blind to the singular, orchestrated concatenation of events leading to the slaughter. The poison is embraced by willing lips, a draught thought to be an expression of now requited love. Too late the lover realizes the duplicity, the mendacity, the truth. The lover was nothing more than an instrument, used by the beloved, for the purposes of the beloved, seen as having no intrinsic value, not an object for respect or admiration––not even an object for recognition, as such, but undeniably an object. For he is no Romeo, nor she Juliet. He will slay her and himself remain alive, alive to profit from the slaying, profit from the machinations, and gloat over the profit. No tears are shed, for the lover realizes the visceral truth too late, and the beloved cannot cry over the perceived nothingness that was once the lover. The wind howls its lament. Those that remain do not have ears to

hear. They will never have ears to hear. Aceldama.[35]
Woe. Woe.

---

[35] From the Aramaic, *hagel dama* (Greek: *Akeldama*). Literally, *field of blood*: the land purchased by Judas with the bribe money he took for betraying Jesus. See Acts 1:18 – 19.

CHAPTER THREE

PEGGY JUST WASN'T THAT KIND OF GIRL

Peggy just wasn't that kind of girl. So it came as a surprise, a shock really, when she found herself in the back seat of the Buick, Larry Sanders on top of her, her dress over her face and her panties bunched up around her ankles. That was in 10th grade, during football season, and since she wasn't that kind of a girl, she didn't tell her best friend Ellen or her second best friend Judy or her longest friend since kindergarten Deloris, or any of the other girls in the band or any of the girls on the cheerleading squad, and she sure wasn't going to tell her sister or her parents--why would she?--and since she wasn't that kind of girl, there was nothing to say. She knew what she believed and she was definitely saving herself for marriage. She remembered most of the Ten Commandments and the sermon on the mount from Sunday school and she knew right from wrong. So she had nothing to say to anybody about the nonevent with Larry. And as far as Larry was concerned, he felt the same way. He had nothing to say to her the next day when they passed in the hallway--almost bumped into each other, really. Larry had a look of horror on his face as he said "pardon me", and took off like his pants were on fire. Peggy felt a little embarrassed too, maybe, but nothing like Larry. They weren't friends, anyway––he was just some guy from Vo-Tech––so she put it out of her mind.

Years later, she looked at Larry's picture in the yearbook like it was a different lifetime: Larry Sanders, Vo-Tech,   and then there was nothing after his name, like Cheerleading 9, 10, 11, 12, Orchestra 9, 10, 11, 12, Track, 10, 11, 12, National Honor Society, Concert Band 9, 10, 11, 12, Fall Play 9,10,11,12, Spring Musical 9,10,11,12, like there was after Peggy's name. She couldn't remember actually speaking to Larry Sanders after the night in the Buick.

All through high school, Peggy used to walk the family dog, a shepherd-Rottweiler-corgi-mutt mix named Dixie, around the almost always deserted county park, mainly since the dog usually stayed inside and had to go out sometime and the park was right next to their house. Nobody she knew hung out there, but two or three times a week she'd take Dixie on a loop around the park after supper.

One day during the summer before 11th grade, she walked past a guy about her age who said "hi" and she said "hi" back and since he was cute and friendly, she took Dixie on an extra lap, a lap on which she met "Doug" from upstate who happened to be visiting some relatives. He was so friendly that she agreed to meet him the next night after supper so they both could talk and walk Dixie.

Peggy was surprised by the coldness of the cement bathroom floor. She had tied Dixie around a tree in a clump of woods and she and Doug had headed for the women's bathroom. It all happened so fast. They were just talking and by the second time around, they were holding hands and by the end of the second time around Doug had asked her into the bathroom and there she was, pants and underpants off, half-crumpled and under her legs, t-shirt and bra somewhere else.

She almost got into a panic when he was on top of her and suddenly she couldn't remember if his name was Doug or Dan. Suddenly, she had the urge to cry but then it was over and Doug or Dan was standing up, pulling up his pants, and holding out his hand to her. All of a sudden she remembered that his name was Doug, Doug from upstate. She walked Dixie every night for the next two weeks, but evidently the D-man must've left town earlier than expected, since she didn't run across him again. Not that it was likely, but Peggy was super glad nobody had walked into the women's room when she was sprawled on the floor with Doug, since they would have for sure gotten the wrong idea. Peggy knew she wasn't that kind of girl.

When Carl asked Peggy if she needed a ride home from school, at first she said no. But then Carl pointed out that it was going to be dark soon, and Peggy changed her mind. It was the spring of her junior year, and both she and Carl were in the pit orchestra for the school musical, *Oliver*. Carl played bassoon and Peggy flute, and even though they sat only one chair apart for a month of rehearsals and shows, Carl hadn't really crossed Peggy's mind, other than "the nerdy bassoon player" two chairs down. So she was almost shocked when she rubbed the palm of her hand along Carl's right thigh as he was driving down Charlotte Street toward her house, almost home.

At first, Carl acted like nothing had happened, so Peggy kept stroking his thigh, closer and closer to his crotch. He parked down the street from her house and turned off the engine, unbuckling his seatbelt. He didn't look at her, but looked straight ahead as he ran his right palm along the inside of her thigh. She thought to herself that this wasn't like her at all, she didn't know what had gotten into her as she began to rub Carl's crotch. It wasn't long before they were both naked in the front seat, and then naked in the back seat, and Peggy realized they hadn't said a word since they hit Charlotte Street. Afterwards, they struggled in silence to get their clothes back on, a task seemingly much more difficult than taking them off. Carl drove her around the block and stopped. She got her flute and books off the floor under the dash and headed up the driveway.

The next rehearsal ended just before dusk. Peggy looked around. Carl had already left the building.

Her senior year, Peggy met Brad at the post-football season band mixer. He was everything she wanted him to be, and more. They were in love. The only tension in their relationship was sexual: he wanted to have sex with her (although he called it making love) and she just wasn't that kind of girl, so she said no.

Brad said he respected her beliefs and that was it. The issue wasn't resolved, but it seemed like it was on hold until the night Peggy invited Brad to come over when Peggy's parents had gone to a concert in town. When he got there, he rang the bell, and Peggy yelled down for him to come on up. She imagined his heart beating with anticipation as he walked up the stairs. He walked into her bedroom and she peeked from the open bathroom door. She wasn't quite ready, she said, but he could sure hang out in her room.

Peggy was standing in front of her bathroom mirror, her back to Brad, in nothing but panties. She looked amazing. Before she knew it, Brad was behind her, gently rubbing her stomach just above the pantyline, and then cupping her breasts. She turned to him and they were on the bed, she untying his sneakers, then pulling down his zipper. Both naked on top on the bedspread, she whispered into his ear: "Be sure to pull out." She never thought about protection, because nothing like this was ever going to happen. She just wasn't that kind of girl.

Brad and Peggy loved each other until they went off to their respective colleges and then, according to all accounts, they lost contact.

It was a whole new world when Peggy got to college. Her parents helped her move into the women's wing of the university dorm. Her roommates Stacy and Nancy seemed cool, so cool in fact that they became friends and hung out together all the time.

The second weekend of their first semester, the three of them went to a party at a frat house and that's where Peggy met Dale. By the end of the night, Dale knew that Peggy lived in the east wing of Goshen Hall, and the night after that, he called the hall phone in that wing asking for Peggy, who happened to be in her room thinking about Dale. Dale asked her to go to the movies on Thursday, right off campus, and of course she agreed. She didn't watch much of the show because she was busy thinking about Dale. She touched his hand in the dark of the theater, and they held hands for the longest time. They held hands as they walked back to her dorm after the movie.

As they said their awkward goodbyes, Peggy moved close to Dale, so close that as she looked up, her lips touched his. There was a short silence, and then Dale asked if she wanted to go see his room at the frat house. Before he had even finished, she agreed, and they held hands as they walked. Peggy felt like they had known each other all their lives. It turned out that, being a junior, Dale had his own room, and it got so late that Peggy didn't want to leave--and Dale didn't want her to leave. So she slept in Dale's bed. They didn't actually make out until the next morning, right before Dale left for his 8:00 class. Peggy didn't want him to go, so she kept opening and closing the bathroom door while he was in there getting dressed, asking him questions, and before she knew it they were both back on the bed and he was lifting her top and kissing her stomach and she was kissing the top of his head.

She didn't see a lot of Stacy and Nancy after that because she was always over at Dale's. She saw even less of her roommates after she got into a big fight with Stacy over Dale because Stacy was telling Peggy that she was missing out on a lot of stuff at college because she was spending so much time with Dale--too much time, according to Stacy. The thing that really irked Peggy was that Nancy was there and heard the whole thing, but she didn't say a word. After that, Peggy basically moved into Dale's room at the frat house, and the brothers seemed cool with it because nobody said a thing.

Everything was copacetic until the spring, when Peggy heard through the grapevine that Dale might have something going on on the side. The rumor turned out to be true.

It was almost like Peggy was the "other girl". Dale's other girlfriend was back in his hometown of Youngstown and never visited campus. It made sense now that he took off early and came back late during every break.

Peggy confronted Dale and there was a big showdown and the fight lasted until Peggy and Dale had sex, about three that morning. She couldn't see herself going back to the dorm with Stacy and Nancy.

Peggy and Dale broke up, so to speak, about a dozen or so times during the last half of the spring semester, but Peggy was always back at the frat house before long, right there in Dale's smallish double bed.

It's hard to say when they broke up for real. Dale had a job in town, so he planned to continue to stay in the frat house for the summer. Peggy wanted to stay with him, but she ended up going back to her old summer job back home in Lancaster and living with her parents. She did call Dale every night, and sometimes in the morning.

About mid-July, he stopped answering and she wasn't able to reach him for four days, so she decided to ask if she could borrow the car and drive back to campus, only to find that when she got to Dale's room in the frat house, she was face to face with another girl, a girl who said she was Dale's girlfriend, a girl who said she never heard of Peggy, a girl who then called her a crazy bitch and told her to get out. Peggy always thought of herself as a girl. The girl got out. She went to a cheap motel just off campus. She called the frat house phone about ten times over the next two days, and then gave up.

She decided to go back home to Lancaster. As she walked to the car, she saw Dale. She didn't know what to do, so she burst into tears and ran away.

Later, she felt vindicated. She knew it was all his fault. He wasn't even good for her, she told herself, especially since he didn't even share her beliefs. He was so lost he didn't even believe in God. She was going to save herself for the right guy. She didn't go out for track in college, but she kept herself up by running most days of the week, two or three miles at a time, and she knew the guys noticed her.

That August, Peggy got her own small efficiency adjacent to the north side of campus. Her parents helped her with the rent. After her experiences with Stacy and Nancy, Peggy had decided that she wanted to have her own place, even if it was only 175 square feet. She felt a new wave of liberation.

She didn't waste any time getting over Dale. She met Dave at band camp, two weeks before her sophomore year at the university. There were a lot of guys to choose from, but she was immediately drawn to him because he paid so much attention to her. It wasn't long before they were inseparable.

Peggy thought Dave was different from all the other guys she had dated. She thought he was the one. He was so sensitive to her needs, and he never thought she was high maintenance. He was so great.

Like the time Peggy was so down about her math

class.   She was so worried that she almost had a breakdown.   She had only met Dave three weeks before.   Dave came over to her place with food and iced tea, and he listened to her express her concerns about the class for a good two hours.

And he wasn't just some guy listening, Peggy realized, because he had had the class the year before and gotten an "A".   The next night and a bunch of nights after that, he even helped her with her homework. He was the best tutor a girl could have.

Peggy knew they were going to have to deal with it when they got to it, but she wasn't going to bring it up because she just wasn't that kind of girl.

Dave brought it up one night late when he was tutoring Peggy on her math.   Dave said he had feelings for Peggy. Peggy said she was saving herself for marriage. It was almost like Dave didn't hear her, but guys are usually like that, Peggy thought. Dave said again that he had feelings for her, so she said that she thought that was wonderful and that she had feelings for him as well. He was nearly beaming, and when he leaned in to give her a kiss, she turned her head and coughed.

Peggy and Dave spent literally every day together during her sophomore year, all except when they visited their respective families. Peggy said she'd take Dave home when the time was right, but it was never right.

They got along great, all except for one gigantic fight in late April. It had to do with sex. Peggy figured it would have to do with sex. They were eating dinner one night. It was pizza from Pie in the Sky, right off campus. They delivered. Peggy wasn't much for cooking, especially with all the classwork. Dave took a bite of the pepperoni pizza and then looked point blank at Peggy and asked her why she never wanted to kiss him.

That in itself made her angry enough, but it was when he asked her if she "maybe liked girls" that she got really pissed off. She was so pissed off that she told him to leave and not come back. She changed her mind by the next day, and since he apologized, she let him come back over and help her study for the math final.

Peggy and Dave never really did officially break up. That summer, she went back home and worked part time and met Phil. He was 31 and manly, with some big tattoos he got overseas when he was in the Navy. He was not at all like shy, pencil-thin Dave. They worked most of the same shifts at the restaurant, so Peggy ended up riding with Phil. He didn't mind picking her up, since it was only a couple of miles out of his way. And besides, he liked Peggy and Peggy liked him.

It wasn't long before Phil invited Peggy over to his place to see his beer can collection. Peggy had assumed that Phil had his own place, but when he pulled up to the garage and pointed up at a bay window above, she realized that he lived over his parent's garage.

The first thing Peggy noticed were the pictures of naked women on the wall behind the bed. Phil noticed that she had noticed, so he asked her what she thought of the pictures. She didn't know what to say, but then she said that she could understand why he liked them. Phil responded by putting his hands on her shoulders and staring her in the eyes. He said that he agreed--every one of the women on the wall was beautiful--but that Peggy was even more beautiful.

Peggy asked him how he would know. Phil said that he'd like to be sure, but that he was never wrong. "I ain't never seen any woman as beautiful as you," he said, smiling. "And I'd like to see everything." Peggy didn't answer. When she did speak, it was to ask him where the bathroom was, although it was obvious that there was only one other door in the place.

He showed her his beer can collection for all of an hour, pointing out some fine details on each can shelved along the south wall. She looked intently although she couldn't think of anything that held less allure. She was in front of him and he rubbed against her back and rear end as he gave the tour. At the end of the shelves, she turned around and they kissed. Before they left, Phil was able to see everything. All summer long, he picked her up for work and dropped her back off at home after stopping by at his place.

After that summer, Peggy didn't see Phil again until the next summer, the summer after her junior year, and by the time she got back to campus that fall, she had forgotten all about Dave. When Dave unexpectedly showed up at her place on the third day back, professing his love for her, she laughed at him and told him he was nuts and didn't know what he was talking about. He didn't leave. Finally, she told him that she was tired and wanted to go to bed. She saw him around campus after that, but they didn't get past hello.

Phil called from Lancaster a few times, but their conversations were never more than five minutes and consisted mostly of awkward silences. Peggy usually told Phil that she'd be back in Lancaster over the summer and they could talk then, but Phil always told her that he "wanted to see everything."

After one such conversation, Peggy remembers telling herself that the best thing about Phil was that he didn't have the gas money to visit her at college.

Her junior year at the university was a dating wasteland. Peggy couldn't seem to get anybody she was interested in interested in her. She spent quite a bit of time on lonely weekends telling herself that this was good for her, that God had a plan for her life, and that she was saving herself for marriage. This message was reinforced by her parents, her mother mostly, who told her that everything happens for a reason and that if Peggy would just have faith, she would be rewarded. Her mother, of course, didn't know about Larry or Doug or Carl or Brad or Dale or Dave or Phil. And she didn't know about Travis.

Peggy met Travis at a convenience store right off campus while she was pumping gas. Travis walked right up to her and asked if he could pump her gas for her, and she, surprised, said yes. It turned out that Travis came from Denver, he said, to attend the university, but his money ran out and he didn't want to take out any more loans, so he was working at an oil change place in Bausman. She remembered him saying that he got straight As in high school and that he had a football scholarship to a NCAA Division I school, but he turned it down because he wanted to concentrate on academics. When she found out that his car was in the shop, she offered to drive him to his place, and he was immediately amenable. Peggy told

Travis all about herself on the way to his place. She even told him about her college art project and how proud she was. "I'd love to see it," Travis said. "I'd really love to see it. Actually, I'm kind of an artist myself." When Peggy heard that, and thought about what her mom always said about everything happening for a reason, she made a left and headed right back to the university. Turned out, Travis really did like her art project. He liked her art project so much that he asked if she would model for him for a project he was working on, a project that he said had already generated some interest. Peggy got excited. It sounded like a great opportunity. Besides, she always felt that she was no ordinary girl, that she was destined for something more.

Travis arrived the next Tuesday, camera in hand. When Peggy mentioned that she thought that she was going to model for his sketches, he said that he did do sketches, but that he was more of a collage multimedia artist and that this part of the project involved photoart. Peggy hesitated, then agreed that he could take nude photos of her, as long as they were "artfully done". He assured her this would certainly be the case. "Maybe you could model for me too" Peggy asked. "Sure, baby, sure," he said. Travis took more than a hundred artfully done nude photos of Peggy, then she donned a bathrobe and made a stick figure sketch of Travis in the nude. Nude Travis jumped to see the newly completed sketch. He liked the sketch so much that he gave Peggy a long hug. She hugged him back and soon the lovemaking on the living room rug began. They never even made it to the bed.

Four days later, Travis called Peggy and told her

that the film was developed and asked her if she would like to see the pictures. She said "Maybe another time".

Travis called for two weeks after that but never was able to reach Peggy. It was then that Peggy consciously got the idea that all men were scum.

Three weeks later, Peggy went back home for the summer, back to her job at the restaurant. She called Phil on her first night back and he picked her up for work the next day. He took her back to his place after work.

By June, Peggy was already getting bored and was half asleep as Phil pulled up to his garage apartment. Peggy thought about breaking up with Phil. They walked up the rickety steps and entered, but before Peggy knew it, there were shouts. Phil was having a surprise 21st birthday party for Peggy! Phil had invited all the other dishwashers and even the short order cooks and waitresses over to his place for the party, and everybody except Ted made it because he was sick, and they had all beaten Peggy and Phil to his place. There were fourteen people in all and they all managed to fit into Phil's place, although he only had four chairs and five milk crates to sit on. Peggy noticed that all the photos of the naked women were gone. Everybody was so nice to Peggy. It was only the second real birthday party she had ever had. She got presents too, and Phil got her a T-shirt ("Can't Do Better Than This"), a bandana, and a bracelet, all matching. He looked like he was having the time of his life. On the way home, Peggy felt depressed. She had asked Phil if he would keep her presents at his place. He took it as a compliment.

The next morning, her Mom asked Peggy how her birthday went, since she didn't see Peggy all day. Peggy said it went fine, but didn't mention the party.

Peggy hadn't seen Ellen, Judy, or Deloris for over a year. She had barely spoken with them on the phone since she went away to college. Peggy couldn't even remember how long it had been. She was dating Dave, that's all she remembers. When they were kids, it would have been unimaginable, going so long without talking. They used to see each other every day at school, and then talk on the phone every night, and they never ran out of things to say. Peggy felt sad.

On her day off, Peggy decided to call Ellen, but she wasn't home. Neither was Judy. Deloris was home and they talked for a good twenty minutes, but it wasn't like old times. Deloris was dating a guy at college named Chuck. They'd been together since freshman year. Peggy told Deloris that she wasn't dating anyone. Peggy and Deloris agreed to get together before the fall semester, but somehow the time got away from them. Ellen's mom must've given her the message that Peggy called because a few weeks later Peggy got a call from Ellen, who apologized two or three times, saying that she just got engaged to her boyfriend Randy and they were busy making plans.

By the time Peggy got back to campus for the start of her senior year, she was sick and disgusted with having sex with Phil, although it amazed her that Phil seemed to be enjoying it more and more all the time. She didn't even like how Phil smelled, and she hated his stupid goatee.

She thanked God that she had never gotten a disease and she knew it had to be more than luck, since she could have been more careful. She decided her first day back that she was going to forget about Phil and move on with her life.

It turned out to be easy for Peggy to forget about Phil. She never had thought about him much, except when she was trying to figure out how to end the relationship. But she never thought about it as a relationship, and that made it that much harder for her to end it. She secretly hoped that Phil would find somebody else and just go away.

By the time Peggy met Greg, Phil seemed like another lifetime. They met in the library. She said hi first, but then when he saw her at the drinking fountain with her books, he asked her how she liked her poly sci class. She thought he was cute and nice. Greg invited Peggy to a Wednesday night Bible study on campus and before she knew it she had agreed to go. She didn't remember where her Bible was, but she found it later in a box on her closet floor.

Peggy's mind wandered during the Bible study. She was thinking about Greg. After Bible study, Peggy hung around to talk with Greg. There were quite a few people, and many stayed around afterwards to talk. Greg saw her and asked her if she wanted to go to the campus café with him and some others. She said yes but then was so bored at the café that she made up an excuse to leave early. Peggy walked the four blocks to her place, feeling depressed. She had hoped to spend some quality time alone with Greg. She realized that she didn't even have his number.

When she got home, Peggy put her Bible back in

the box on the closet floor. She lay on her bed and stared, then picked up the phone and called Phil. No answer. She realized he was still at the restaurant. She left him a message to call back, no matter how late. She was still awake when he called at 12:45.

It was a good thing he took the lead, because Peggy had no idea what to do. Peggy figured that Phil wasn't as dumb as she thought he was. He was sure she called for phone sex. She denied it. He claimed that she never called him unless she wanted a ride, and she didn't want a ride, so she must want sex. And then he went so far as to tell Peggy that that was a good thing. She told him his mind was in the gutter. Then he asked her why she called, if it wasn't for sex. After a long silence, he told her he wanted to see everything. They had phone sex. Afterwards, Phil thanked Peggy. Peggy told Phil that it was a one-time thing, but Peggy ended up calling Phil two-dozen or so more times during the fall semester of her senior year, all the way up until the day she met Tony.

It was just Peggy's luck to meet Tony during finals week and then have to spend the four-week Christmas break thinking about him. She was at the university café, sitting by herself, feeling so lonely that it hurt, trying to cram for her econ final and trying not to think about calling Phil. She always crammed at the end of the semester because her mind was always too scattered to actually sit down and do any studying, unless it was an emergency. Peggy knew her 2.9 GPA didn't really reflect her ability, but she was usually so distracted that she was thankful that it wasn't even lower. She kept trying not to think about calling Phil.

She generally thought more about trying not to

think about Phil than she did about Phil, but after Tony sat down she forgot about Phil, calling Phil, and her econ final.

Peggy was minding her own business, trying to concentrate. Then she looked up and there he was. Tony seemed so suave that Peggy couldn't help but stare. She told herself that it wasn't polite, but her eyes felt glued to Tony's. Instead of walking past, he sat right down beside Peggy, who promptly made a fool of herself. "What planet are you from?" she blurted out, much too loud for the university library during finals week. It was a good thing that Tony took it as a good thing. He smiled and asked her how the econ was going. She continued her stupid streak (she thought in retrospect) by saying she had forgotten all about it. Tony continued to smile. She thought for a minute that he might be noticing her breasts and torso. Her tight top was paying off. Peggy knew her looks weren't beauty-pageant, that she only had what most girls had, but she milked it for all she could.

There was an awkward silence. Tony kept smiling at Peggy and Peggy kept smiling at Tony. Peggy thought there must be a deeper connection. Nothing happens by accident, she thought. And God only helps those who help themselves. "Are you good at econ?" asked Peggy, finally. "I can be if you need me to be," said Tony. He was still smiling. "I need you to be. I can't concentrate in here. Can you help me at my place?" Her heart was pounding. She knew it was bold, even for her. "You know I can. When? My name's Tony, by the way." "Peggy. So nice to meet you. How about now. Now would be good."

Peggy felt her insides burn with excitement. The last thing she felt was lonely and she forgot all about calling Phil.

As Peggy and Tony headed across campus to her place, they bumped into Dave. Nobody spoke. Peggy remembered Dave tutoring her in math sophomore year. She had forgotten about him. She laughed to herself as she thought about how much Tony was not going to tutor her in econ.

Tony asked Peggy a bunch of questions about herself on the walk over to her place, but she didn't ask him a thing. She really didn't feel like talking. She gave Tony short but polite answers and wondered why he cared. He seemed like a nice guy, but so what? she thought. There are a million nice guys out there, but in the end you end up alone.

Peggy knew she wasn't any good at econ. But she was good at something. With more practice, she hoped she would get even better. She opened her front door, turned, grabbed Tony by his belt buckle, and pulled him in. He was still smiling.

It was nearly nineteen years later when Peggy ran into Phil at Wade's discount grocery on the east side of Lancaster. Even after so long, there was instant recognition. It turned out that they were living only blocks apart. Peggy told Phil that she still hadn't found "Mr. Right" and frankly, she was sick of looking. Phil smiled and said he had had a few false starts but now he was single again. Then he asked her if she wanted to see his beer can collection.

Driving over to his place, they joked about old times.

QUESTIONS:

(1) What kind of a person is Peggy?

(2) Would you want to be friends with Peggy? Why or why not?

(3) What does Peggy *think* her moral beliefs are? (Her ideal belief system, what she tells herself she believes).

(4) What are Peggy's *actual* moral beliefs? That is, if you go by behavior alone, what are Peggy's moral beliefs?

(5) Is there a difference between what Peggy's moral beliefs are and what Peggy thinks her moral beliefs are? If so, how is this possible? Explain.

(6) Finally, if Peggy came to you for advice because she was depressed and she told you that her life wasn't going the way she had planned, what advice would you give her?

CHAPTER FOUR

WHAT WOULD JESUS DO?

An American dies every 12 minutes as a result of not having health insurance. According to a Harvard University Medical School and Cambridge Health Alliance study, 45,000 Americans die every year because they don't have health insurance.[36]

More Americans die every year as a direct result of not having health insurance than have died in all combined terrorist attacks in the history of the United States. Given an average life expectancy of 78.7 years,[37] 3,541,500 Americans will die during an average individual's lifetime because they don't have health insurance.

---

[36] *American Journal of Public Health*, 2009 (http://ajph.aphapublications.org/).

See David Cecere, Cambridge Health Alliance, *Harvard Gazette*, September 7, 2009. Accessible at http://news.harvard.edu/gazette/story/2009/09/new-study-finds-45000-deaths-annually-linked-to-lack-of-health-coverage/ .

[37] National Center for Health Statistics, United States Department of Health and Human Services, 2010 data. See also the Centers for Disease Control and Prevention data at http://www.cdc.gov/nchs/fastats/lifexpec.htm .

The United States is currently ranked 53rd in life expectancy, with a much lower life expectancy than many other industrialized nations. See http://www.geoba.se/population.php?pc=world&type=015&year=2013&st=rank&asde=&page=1 .

See also World Health Organization data at http://www.who.int/gho/mortality_burden_disease/life_tables/situation_trends/en/ .

This number is more than double the number of U.S. service personnel killed in all wars in the history of the United States.[38] Put differently, 841% more Americans currently die each year as a result of not having health insurance than die as a result of military combat operations.[39] If this isn't systemic violence against the citizens of the United States, what is? If this isn't a form of domestic terrorism, what is? If this is a civilization, what isn't? 3,541,500 of your fellow citizens will die during your lifetime as a result of not having health insurance.[40] This is the best we can do? This is loving your neighbor as yourself?[41] Really?

---

[38] The number of U.S. service personnel killed in all wars in the history of the United States is, roughly, 1.321 million, which is only 37% of the number of Americans who die during an average person's lifetime as a result of not having health insurance. See the militaryfactory.com statistics at http://www.militaryfactory.com/american_war_deaths.asp .

[39] Over the course of our nation's history, an average of 5,348 military personnel were killed per year (11% of the number who currently die each year as a result of not having health insurance).

[40] That is, if you don't die prematurely as a result of not having health insurance but live 78.7 years.

[41] See Luke 10:25–37. The Parable of the Good Samaritan.

CHAPTER FIVE

TRUTH IS WHAT PASSES FOR TRUTH

It happened on Super Bowl Sunday, 2012. Those that were there were at odds concerning what to do. One of them––we'll call him Waylon––decided to contact me. After listening to the lengthy saga, I noted that it posed a number of more-or-less thorny moral issues, so I decided to recount it here. The best way to tell the story, in my estimation, would be for Waylon to tell it himself––in his own words––so that is precisely what follows.

*   *   *   *   *

It was Super Bowl Sunday, 2012. My wife Phyllis and I went to church for the 9:00 Sunday service as usual. The sermon was unusually good. Pastor Jill dressed up as a football referee––she even had a whistle, which she blew at the end of the sermon. She talked about football. Like I said, the sermon was unusually good––so good, in fact, that both Phyllis and I took note.

On the twenty-minute drive home, Phyllis and I talked about the sermon and how good it was. Not the typical, one-point simple-as-pie thing we usually got. It occurred to me that maybe, just maybe the sermon wasn't wholly a product of Pastor Jill, that maybe, just maybe she had had a little help on it. I kept the thought to myself, but right before we pulled into the driveway, Phyllis blurted out, "I don't think that was Pastor Jill's sermon. I don't think that was her sermon at all." I parked and we just sat there.

"I was basically thinking the same thing," I said. "Maybe she had a little help, or maybe she just worked extra hard on it. Or ––you never know––maybe the spirit was really speaking to her this week. We can't rule that out." Phyllis looked at me with this look of downright incredulousness that said it all.

"What if she did get some help? How are we gonna know, anyway?" I said. "Let's talk about it later, OK? I want to get going on the food," Phyllis said. We had three other couples coming over for the game. "OK. Sure." I went upstairs to change. It wasn't ten minutes later that Phyllis showed up in the bedroom with something she printed off the computer. She handed it to me and I started reading. After a paragraph, I had to sit down. There it was––the entire sermon right off some preacher-aid website, with the exact same title and everything. I wouldn't have believed it, so I had to sit there and read through the whole thing twice. Every word was there. The complete sermon was stolen from some Internet website, and I had just listened to it for 15 minutes not a hour before. It was a weird feeling. I felt like I was being lied to. Phyllis wasn't so keen on it either. And since she was on the Pastor-Parish Relations Committee, she was going to bring it up.

The next Pastor-Parish Relations Committee meeting ended up being about a month or so later. Phyllis had already discussed the lifted sermon with one of the five other people on the committee, and that person was as appalled as she.

She presented her findings to the small committee, a thing made all that much more difficult by the fact that Pastor Jill was right there at the meeting with the other five.

What followed was what I can only describe as a rather disturbing scene. After Phyllis presented the clear evidence for the 100% lifted--or one might say plagiarized--sermon, she thought there might be some kind of an admission--if not an admission of guilt, at least an admission of having passed something off as one's own that wasn't. But that's not what happened. That's not what happened at all. The pastor denied having done anything wrong, stating that she was merely doing what she had learned to do from her mentor, the mentor that had guided her in the ways of pastoring, the mentor who had guided her in the ways of shepherding the flock.

Some of the committee members commiserated with Pastor Jill, stating that when they had occasion to give a lay sermon, they might look to books or the Internet for a little inspiration and guidance. Phyllis carefully explained once again that it was a little more than mere inspiration and that the entire sermon was taken right off some preacher website. One more person finally got it. But for the other three, there seemed to be no comprehension of what Phyllis was saying. Three of the four committee members who were hearing the information for the first time simply dismissed it out of hand, since, in their minds (1) The pastor could never have done such a thing, therefore (2) Phyllis must have gotten it wrong, therefore (3) There was no need to look at the specious "evidence" and spread false rumors. Subsequently, the matter was tabled and that was the end of it.

Needless to say, Phyllis and I have never been able to listen to one of Pastor Jill's sermons in the same way since.

Doing the wrong thing and then doing the wrong thing to cover up doing the wrong thing just doesn't seem like the right thing to do. Especially for someone who is paid to lead the flock of the faithful. But it is 2012. Maybe I've got it all wrong and seeming is what passes for being. I don't know. But Phyllis and I both feel differently about going to church since the incident. Whatever was there before seems to be gone for us. I guess we thought that the pastor would speak from her experience, from her walk with God, from her careful and fearful study, meditation and prayer.

But it turns out that it was more like a performance, a performance we continue to pay for quite handsomely week after week. Are we simply paying to hear what we want to hear? Maybe, but since Phyllis downloaded the complete Super Bowl Sunday sermon from some crummy website, I've been wondering a lot about the truth. If I support someone lying to me from the pulpit week after week, what does that say about me?

Maybe Phyllis and I would have been better off being like three of the six members of the Pastor-Parish Relations Committee--just don't even entertain the notion that the Pastor could be making stuff up, or ripping stuff off. After all, isn't belief all about deciding what you want to believe? Why couldn't we just decide what to believe about this too? Couldn't we just decide to trust Pastor Jill, and if she lifted a sermon or two from the Internet, she must have a good reason, right? She must know what she is doing, right? Maybe that is right. But all I know is that Phyllis and I have been having a harder and harder time going back to church to listen to Pastor Jill. We feel like somehow we are knowingly participating in a fraudulent enterprise, and it feels bad. Should we try to quell the doubts and live by faith, or should we follow what we know is true and alter our behavior accordingly? What would you do? Anyway, thanks for listening.

*   *   *   *   *

Like I said at the beginning, Waylon came to me with the story of Pastor Jill. He was seeking moral guidance. If he came to you, what kind of guidance do you think you could provide? Here are a few questions I think germane to this issue, questions that must be answered prior to any constructive course of action:

(1)   Did Pastor Jill do anything morally wrong in "borrowing" an entire sermon from a website? (Note that philosophical ethics and theological ethics may not be compatible, and they may not be reducible to the same

answer. On the other hand, they are not necessarily incompatible).

(2) If Pastor Jill did do something morally wrong, what was it, and why was it wrong?

(3) If you were in Waylon and Phyllis' situation, how do you think you would feel? Why?

(4) If you were in Waylon and Phyllis' situation, what do you think you would do, if anything? Why?

(5) Imagine that you are graduating from college. The commencement speaker delivers a rousing twenty-minute speech. A week later, you are surfing the Internet and find that the speech given by the speaker at your commencement was in fact written in 1967 by a civil rights leader. It becomes evident to you that the commencement speech, in its entirety, was "borrowed" material. You feel disgusted but are not sure why. You call your best friend from college, knowing she was there too, having graduated in the same class. You tell her about your discovery. Her words: "Big deal. Does anybody really care? It was a good speech, wasn't it?" You begin to second guess your first gut reaction. How is this situation similar to the situation with Pastor Jill? How is it dissimilar?

(6) "After all, isn't belief all about deciding what you want to believe? Why couldn't we just decide what to believe about this too?" Is belief a matter of simply deciding what you want to believe? What about evidence for warranted belief? If belief is simply a matter

of deciding what you want to believe, does that mean you get to decide what counts as evidence too? If so, how can any belief ever be "true"?

CHAPTER SIX

IN A PERFECT WORLD THIS BOOK WOULD NOT EXIST

In a perfect world this book would not exist. But existence is an imperfection.[42] Given this, there is something here to disappoint everyone. For example, if you want answers, you'll be disappointed. If you want things to be explicable, you'll be aggravated. If you want something that'll go down easy, you'll be positively disgusted. In other cases, you may simply be appalled. On the other hand, if you want hope, you may find it here. If you want truth, you may also find it. In the end, it just might be that you will find what you want to find. But it will not be spelled out for you; it will be a function of your own journey as you travel a new path that is only for you, a path that only you can take. What other path is truly worthy of your footsteps?

This book is published in a series of essays, but the story is singular. Many chapters can stand alone, but the totality is greater than the sum of its parts. Having said this and knowing that the work addresses multiple issues, do not hesitate to read what you will. A partial narrative may be sufficient for some readers, or a narrative constructed in a wholly different order.

---

[42] Jean-Paul Sartre, *Nausea*, trans. Lloyd Alexander (New York: New Directions, 1964). The French existentialist's most famous novel, first published in 1938.

Chapter 14, PSALM 151: IMPRECATORY (from my forthcoming series of novels *The Terror of the Simulacra*)[43], for example, can be read by itself, without any understanding of the plot or characters found in the trilogy. You are responsible for the subtextuality and the metatextuality, as these are imaginative constructs, and my hope is that you will develop them within the paradigm of your own background and sympathies. Any real constructs must be developed as a function of existential conditions on the ground, as it were, rather than being merely epiphenomena of abstract theory. Your own thoughts and feelings must be the starting point, not a book, a creed, a history, a narrative from outside. This book is but one artifact among many that you may use to understand our present civilization (such as it is). Potentially, you may also use this artifact to build something of lasting value for future civilizations, if such civilizations are to experience the privilege of coming into existence (something that, we all know, is by no means guaranteed). Note the unstated assumptions, suppressed premises, and arguments in the text, as well as the missing narratives. For all narratives are plural, even if cast in the singular. This narrative has an end and at the same time no end, since the end is merely the beginning of what will come next. What will come next is up to you. In these important senses, many and varied demands are placed upon you as the reader of the text.

---

[43] Ross Channing Reed, *The Terror of the Simulacra*, Ozark Mountain Writers Guild, forthcoming.

At this point, you may wonder what this book is about. In the final analysis, you are the subject of this book. This book is about you, the life you live, the people you know, and the choices you make.

How can this book be about you if you have heretofore had no relation to the text? But you do, in fact, have a relation to the text. And it is not really about the text. Think about it. The book is a tool that you may use to address some of the exigencies of your life.

As you know, the use of any tool involves certain risks. Prepare and equip yourself for these risks, and go about the business of caring for yourself and your planet. Every sentient living organism requires care and guidance, a care and guidance that you may both give and receive. May this book serve you in some small capacity as you endeavor to meet this formidable challenge and responsibility.

CHAPTER SEVEN

IT TAKES A KILLING

When I sat down in the late summer of 2008 to write the introduction to *Love and Death: An Existential Theory of Addiction,*[44] the Department of Defense had reported that 4,150 U.S. soldiers had died in Iraq, and over 25,000 had been wounded[45] and the research organization National Priorities Project[46] had reported that U.S. war expenditures in Iraq were ticking away at just over 531 billion dollars, not including the costs to Iraq, other "coalition" forces, or the cleanup costs (to say nothing of the universal loss of goodwill and trust). Reuters UK had reported (January 30, 2008) on the London-based Opinion Research Business study that calculated that 1,033,000 civilians had been killed in the conflict in Iraq.   What might the numbers be today?

To adequately address this question, we would, arguably, need to add the numbers from other conflicts as well, since according to our government, the defined space of the battlefield now includes the

---

[44] Ross Channing Reed, *Love and Death: An Existential Theory of Addiction* (Bloomington, IN: Xlibris, 2009).

[45] The United States Department of Defense, at www.icasualties.org .

[46] www.nationalpriorities.org .

entire planet. To the numbers in Iraq, we would need to add the numbers in the 139 month old war in Afghanistan, as well as the numbers from the undeclared drone strikes in Iraq, Afghanistan, Yemen, Pakistan, Somalia and the Philippines.

Let's begin by looking at the numbers in Iraq and Afghanistan. To date, the Department of Defense reports that 4,486 U.S. soldiers have been killed and 32,223 U.S. soldiers have been wounded in Iraq, and 2,255 U.S. soldiers have been killed and 17,674 U.S. soldiers have been wounded in Afghanistan.[47] The total number of (only) U.S. military casualties (killed and wounded) in both wars is now 56,638. These numbers do not include the horrific psychological toll and resultant mental illnesses suffered by ten of thousands of our troops. The number of civilian casualties is seemingly incalculable, as no reliable numbers appear to be available. Raed Jarrar of the American-Arab Anti-Discrimination Committee puts the calculated death number at 1.2 million Iraqis[48]

The current cost of the wars in Iraq and Afghanistan, based on congressional appropriations, is now $1,480,000,000,000 according to the National Priorities Project[49], enough money to hire 20.3 million elementary school teachers for a year, or to give Pell Grants worth $5550 each to 15 million students for the next 17 years. (National Priorities Project). Or, we could have provided Veterans Administration medical

---

[47] See the current Department of Defense statistics at www.icasualties.org .

[48] Raed Jarrar, "We've Lost Our Country: An Iraqi American Looks Back on a Decade of War That's Devastated a Nation," March 19, 2013 interview at http://www.democracynow.org/2013/3/19/weve_lost_our_country_an_iraqi .

[49] See www.costofwar.com .

care for all veterans for the next 12 years.

For only $204.73 billion (less than 14% of the current costs of the wars in Iraq and Afghanistan) we could have converted 121 million households to renewable solar photovoltaic power—effectively taking all residential housing units off the fossil fuel-hydro-nuclear electric power grid. And these numbers do not, of course, include the full military budget, nor the cost of caring for tens of thousands of injured soldiers who come back stateside and stand (if they are able to stand) in increasingly long lines waiting for benefits. Political Science Professor Neta Crawford of Boston University and Co-Director of the Costs of War Project has calculated, on the tenth anniversary of the invasion, that known costs for the Iraq war were 2.2 trillion, but since the money was borrowed, the interest on the 2.2 trillion will, in the end, exceed the original amount of 2.2 trillion––making the total cost over $4.4 trillion.[50] That's over $14,000 per American. For a family of four, this works out to $56,000––and even this number is an underrepresentation, since, as previously noted, it does not include otherwise allocated military costs nor future health care expenses for our veterans.[51]

Let's take just one family as an example. If 45 year old Larry and 42 year old Tina don't pay for the military spending and instead defer payment until 12 year old Billy and 10 year old Chelsea are adults, the $56,000 could balloon to nearly $80,000 in only ten years, even at the low interest rate of 4%.   So much

[50] http://costsofwar.org/ . (Not to be confused with the previously mentioned site www.costofwar.com).

See also interview with Professor Crawford at http://www.democracynow.org/2013/3/19/the_costs_of_war_10_years .

for an affordable college education for the next generation.[52] And the monetary costs are doubtless the least of all. We will never know all that we have lost. If we had any idea of all that we have lost, of all that we have lost at our own hands, we would go mad with suffering. We would clamor for unconsciousness, oblivion, unbornness.

One debacle like this, one decade long war, is enough to set you back for a lifetime––and that's if you are one of the lucky ones who manages to live thorough it. Tens of thousands of others weren't so lucky. And most of those who weren't so lucky were simply minding their own business, trying to raise their families and earn a living, trying to stay out of the fray of a conflict they couldn't understand. And of those who weren't so lucky, they were on both "sides" of the conflict and they never knew one another and had not a trace of animosity toward one another and had no thought to harm one another and yet they were the unlucky ones. We, the living, as it were, are the lucky ones.

---

[51] The final number per American if these additional costs are added is certainly a matter for debate. A reasonable estimate might put the all-inclusive total cost of military spending per American since the beginning of the Iraq war (including the Iraq and Afghan wars, undeclared wars and drone strikes in Libya, Pakistan, Yemen, Somalia, hundreds of military bases and tens of thousands of troops stationed around the world, and health care costs for wounded and non-wounded veterans) at double the above number, or $28,000 per American. If we add the cost per American for the "too big to fail" bailouts ($17,500,000,000,000 divided by 315,000,000) we arrive at $83,555 per American (which is financed federal debt). See Chapter Six: Zero Sum Hunger Game for a longer treatment of this issue.

[52] Clearly unaffordable for most now, the situation will become increasingly dire, as what's left of the middle class will no longer be able to afford even a state university education (state in name only, as state funding becomes increasingly marginalized). This topic must be the subject of a longer exposé at a later time. Suffice it to say that expenses for higher education have become obscene as our society shifts the costs to students themselves—and peddles predatory loans to "help" make the dream of a higher education and all that it represents come true.

And if only the death and carnage were things of the past. But alas, we know they are not. We know that death and carnage are the soul of the soulless endless present, the soulless endless present of the postindustrial, postmodern, posthuman world, the world that we have created with starry eyes and platitudes of liberation. We could not create *ex nihilo*, no, we told ourselves this had already been done. Since existence, per se, is an imperfection,[53] we denied existence by embracing the ideal, the perfect, the unreal, the imaginary.[54] We end in an empty room, talking only to ourselves. We do not listen.

I could go on with what we are not getting with our blood and money,[55] or continue to enumerate the sacrifices that have been made to create the world that we have now created, but I'd rather ask a few simple questions: What are we doing? Why are we doing it? Who benefits? And is it worth it to those who are making the sacrifices? No one knows when we will have lost our way forever.

Let's pause for a minute to think about the number one American export to the rest of the globe (no, it's not freedom and democracy): weapons sales. In 2011, the United States sold 84 F-15SA fighter jets (and upgraded 70 more) to Saudi Arabia for $29,400,000,000--the largest arms deal on earth since the end of the Cold War.[56]

---

[53] Jean-Paul Sartre, *Nausea*, trans. Lloyd Alexander (New York: New Directions, 1964).

[54] Cf. Ross Channing Reed, *The Terror of the Simulacra*, Ozark Mountain Writers Guild, 2014.

[55] And the blood and money of so many nameless others.

Saudi Arabia is no democracy and makes no pretense of being so. Rather, it is effectively a dictatorship, a royal dictatorship run by The House of Saud.

According to the Central Intelligence Agency, fifteen of the nineteen hijackers on September 11, 2001 were Saudi Arabian.[57] Fifteen of the nineteen hijackers on 9-11 were Saudis and our number one buyer of weapons is Saudi Arabia? Does this make sense to you?

American overseas weapons sales accounted for 77.7% of all international weapons sales in 2011. Let me say it again: American overseas weapon sales accounted for 77.7% of all international weapons sales in 2011. A country with 4.7% of the world's population--the United States of America-- currently sells 77.7% of the world's weapons, a number that is 1653% above the global per capita average.[58]

What kind of civilization have we become--if we are a civilization?[59]

---

[56] Stockholm International Peace Research Institute (http://www.sipri.org/) as reported in *Harper's*, June 2012.

[57]　　　See　　　https://www.cia.gov/news-information/speeches-testimony/2002/DCI_18_June_testimony_new.pdf . These facts were reported in *USA Today*, February 6, 2002.

[58] Thom Shanker, "U.S. Arms Sales Make Up Most of Global Market," *New York Times*, August 26, 2012. Accessible at http://www.nytimes.com/2012/08/27/world/middleeast/us-foreign-arms-sales-reach-66-3-billion-in-2011.html?_r=0 .

[59] See Chapter 15: "Terrorism as a Tool of the International Power Elite". Here Dr. Rutherford Urias Augustus Winter, a character in the novel *The Terror of the Simulacra*, argues that The United States does not meet the necessary preconditions (minimum standards) for a civilization. Even if one argued that the necessary preconditions for a civilization were in fact met, one would be hard pressed to call this civilization free and/or democratic. What conditions are preconditions for a *civi*lization? This should be a matter for open and ongoing public debate—with all perspectives welcome at the table.

Clearly, in our dominant position, we lead the world. What kind of leadership do we exemplify?[60] What kind of world are we creating? Why? Is this what you want for your children?   Your neighbor's children?   Your friends? Your community?

Do we merely lie with the merchants of death out of a craven fear that this is what we have to do to survive, clearly signaling that survival at all costs is the highest ideal? Or do we seek higher ground? Do we seek the light or do we, filled with horror and despondency, turn to calling the darkness light?   Or have we given up on the light altogether? One minute of real living and we know that there is light to be found within the darkness, and even the darkest night portends its dawn.

QUESTIONS:

(1) Discuss the issue of human rights in light of war and weapons sales. Utilize the *United States Constitution* (specifically, the *Bill of Rights*)[61] and the *United Nations Universal Declaration of Human Rights.*[62]

(2) What ethical issues are raised by the preceding numbers regarding casualties in

---

[60] If the best form of leadership is to lead by example, we are creating a world in which surveillance and killer drones will exist in every available worldwide airspace. The ubiquitousness and omniscience of drones will be rivaled only by the Almighty, producing terror forever and ever, amen. As we deny all privacy and grant ourselves the role of judge, jury and executioner, we transcend our mere humanity. We transcend the law, we become the law, we inscribe the law through terror. We become the executioners of both God, the God concept, and finally, humanity as such. Cf. Friedrich Nietzsche, *The Gay Science* (1882), trans. Walter Kaufmann (New York: Vintage, 1974)—in particular, the section titled "The Madman". Cf. also Chapter 14 of the current work, "Psalm 151: Imprecatory".

[61] Accessible at http://constitutionus.com/ .

[62] Accessible at www.un.org/en/documents/udhr .

Iraq and Afghanistan (and the undeclared "secret" drone wars around the world)?

(3)   What ethical issues are raised by the preceding account of the costs of the wars in Iraq and Afghanistan (as well as future conflicts)?

(4)   Is declaring a global war on "insurgents" or "enemy combatants" the best way to protect and defend democracy? Explain.

(5)   What are some of the nonnegotiable aspects of a civilization and why are they essential? Explain.

(6)   What is terrorism? Attempt to give your own working definition of terrorism. Based upon your definition, are drone attacks a form of terrorism? Explain.

CHAPTER EIGHT

ZERO SUM HUNGER GAME

"Between 2007 and 2009, Wall Street profits swelled by 720 percent, even while unemployment rates doubled and home equity dropped by 35 percent. Since 1979, the bottom 90 percent of the nation has consistently lost money while the upper classes have gained. If the average person's wages had kept pace with the economy since the 70s, most people would be making $92,000 per year. The fact is that the upper classes really are taking money from the poor in a very real and concrete way."

Who is speaking here? Some idealistic left-wing liberal fanatic looking for a handout? In fact, no, it's Alan Dunn, writing for the well-known business magazine *Forbes*.[63]

---

[63] Alan Dunn, "Average American v. the One Percent," *Forbes*, March 21, 2012. Accessible   at http://www.forbes.com/sites/moneywisewomen/2012/03/21/average-america-vs-the-one-percent/ .

See also Robert Gebeloff and Shaila Dewan, "Measuring the Top 1% by Wealth, Not Income, *New York Times*, January 17, 2012. Accessible at http://economix.blogs.nytimes.com/2012/01/17/measuring-the-top-1-by-wealth-not-income/ .

Dunn goes on to point out that the top 1% of the American population have an average wealth of $8.4 million, which is 70 times the average net worth of the bottom 99%.[64] 70 times? This means that the average net worth for the bottom 99% is $120,000. But wait. We've got to add in all the sources of debt to get the real numbers, including mortgages, home equity lines of credit ("second mortgages"), student loans, credit cards, auto loans, business debt and local, state, and federal debt that will have to be paid by every American--now or later. You've got to subtract the debits after you add the credits, right? This is fairly simple math--if you can get the numbers. When we do the math with all of these enormous (mostly negative) numbers, you will realize that we are beyond a crisis.

A recent story on National Public Radio may give one an indication of the magnitude of the crisis. Zoe Chace did a story on "Why More People Are Renting Tires".[65] I don't know about you, but the very title of the story really made me think. *More* people renting tires? I didn't even know there was such a thing as tire rental. I mean, if you can't afford tires, you can't afford to drive, right?

Pretty naïve, apparently. It seems that there are a growing number of working poor who need a vehicle to get to work (especially since, for the vast majority

---

[64] And these numbers are based on a 2007 study by the Federal Reserve. See http://www.federalreserve.gov/econresdata/scf/scf_2007.htm . The economic disparity between the rich and the poor has continued to worsen since 2007.

[65] Zoe Chace, "Why More People Are Renting Tires," *Morning Edition*, National Public   Radio,   June   14,   2013.   Accessible   at http://www.npr.org/blogs/money/2013/06/14/191379313/why-more-people-are-renting-tires . The "rental" scheme discussed is really a lease-purchase program.

of Americans, no real public transportation is available), but they can't afford a vehicle to get to work. Thus, the entrepreneur sees a need and fills it.

A new market niche for the socially conscious entrepreneur--renting things to people who can't afford them but need them to live, tire rental being but one of those things. The tires in the story ended up costing twice the retail price, reflecting the 140% markup rental fee.[66] Meanwhile, the 1% has a bigger share of the pie every year. How long will it be before average people will no longer be able to afford to work because wages will simply be too low?[67] What then? Or are we already there?

In a real, concrete sense, the ship (commandeered by the 1%) has already gone down, and soon we will realize that we have lost everything. Almost. What we have not lost is the possibility of regaining the capacity to think for ourselves about the rules of the game we have been playing and, in particular, why we have been playing it. Although we are ostensibly discussing economics, the question of why is not fundamentally an economic question: it is more about who we are as a people. It is about what we value and why we value it. It is, at root, a philosophical question, an ethical question, not a one of technology, logistics, or economic, social or political

---

[66] If drivers can't afford tires, one may also wonder what else they can't afford. Car insurance? Vehicle registration? Vehicle inspection (in states where it is still required)? Driver's license? Basic vehicle maintenance (to ensure safety)? Even fuel could be a problem—indicated by the dramatic increase in vehicle "drive offs" after pumping gas. The silent and not-so-silent desperation is all around us.

[67] Clearly, such people will need to work. The question is whether they can actually sell their labor (increasingly at two or three or four part-time-no-benefit jobs) for enough money to actually live. No wonder the stress level here in the land of the free has reached epic—and epidemic—proportions.

policy.   The issue concerns how we should live together--something squarely in the province of ethics--and what kind of a society we wish to create and transfer to our children. It is a matter concerning how we can live well as a people, with a measure of peace and equilibrium--what Aristotle famously referred to 2400 years ago in his *Nicomachean Ethics* as *eudaimonia*, a concept now often translated simply as "happiness".[68] What could be a more fundamental in the history of human civilization than the question of happiness? Arguably, the majority of those who have ever lived were simply fighting for their lives. Clearly, the same is the case today, even with postindustrial opulence and seemingly boundless prosperity--for a few.   With slogans of freedom, democracy, and human rights ringing in our ears, conditions on the ground have remained essentially the same: the great preponderance of wealth is held by a tiny minority while everyone else scrapes to make ends meet. Any temporary rise in the "middle class" was simply an anomaly: it won't be long before things return to business as usual.   As the ship was

---

[68]   Aristotle,   *Nicomachean   Ethics*,   second   edition,   trans.   Terence   Irwin. Indianapolis: Hackett, 1999. See Book I, 1-18. Aristotle begins this classic work by noting that we all aim at "the good" and that the good at which we aim is meant, *in our own estimation*, to be the route to our ultimate final end or goal (*telos* in Greek) of *eudaimonia* (or, roughly translated, happiness, or living well).   We all seek happiness by making choices that we think are "good". But Aristotle then goes on to caution that although we cannot help but seek that which we *think* is good, most people are in fact mistaken about the good and so end up seeking things that hurt them (and, by extension, hurt others as well).   The key, Aristotle maintains, is to come to know what the good really is, and this is only possible if we live a life of virtue (He claims that we need a model or mentor in order to truly learn how to live an ethical life). The only way to be truly happy, Aristotle argues, is to live an ethical life, a life in accord with our true nature and desires, not a life based on a delusion about who we really are as human beings. True self-knowledge is indispensable. Simply put, we cannot kill, imprison, torture, terrorize, surveil, repress, silence, lie, crush or drone our way to peace, equilibrium, happiness. At least, not according to Aristotle.

going down (subsequent to the 2008 "financial collapse" of Wall Street banks), a silent transfer of wealth was taking place (through the U.S. Treasury and the Federal Reserve Bank) from you to the 1%.[69] According to Nomi Prins, former managing director at Goldman Sachs, the real bailout numbers were between $13.3 trillion and $17.5 trillion[70]. Nomi Prins and Christopher Hayes, writing for *The Nation*[71] put the bailout number at $17.5 trillion, which works out to $55,555 for every man, woman and child in the United States (and rising), or $222,222 for a family of four-- 38.7 times the savings of the average American

---

[69] In fact, the transfer went to a select subset of the 1%, something more on the order of 0.1%. And—the bailouts are not over. The Federal Reserve is still at it, effectively off the radar of most Americans. See Rana Foroohar, "The Housing Mirage," *Time,* May 20, 2013, 18. Accessible at http://www.time.com/time/magazine/article/0,9171,2143008,00.html . Foroohar echoes others in maintaining that our current situation is one of "prerecovery": "It's worth keeping in mind that this prerecovery has been underwritten by the government at historically unprecedented levels. Every month, the Federal Reserve is purchasing $40 billion worth of mortgage-backed securities." Every month? That's $127 for every single American every single month, year after year ($1524 per American per year), with no end in sight? Why the Wall Street welfare? What is it about this situation that we don't know? There certainly could be other solutions to move America from prerecovery to recovery. Why doesn't the Federal Reserve simply give each American $127 per month? For a family of four, this would be $6096 per year, every single year, with no end it sight... That's exactly what we're doing right now, only you're not getting the money. And the bigger question: why a private central bank in the first place? This is a private bank undemocratically setting monetary policy for an entire nation. What's wrong with this picture? For more on this, see Nomi Prins, *It Takes A Pillage: An Epic Tale of Power, Deceit, and Untold Trillions* (Hoboken, NJ: John Wiley and Sons, 2011), Chapter 5: "We Already Have a Bad Bank: It's Called the Federal Reserve," 100–132.

Recently, there has been a (nonpublic) debate concerning whether to limit or curtail the Fed's "bond-buying stimulus" and the press is reporting that the Federal Reserve's current monthly purchases are not $40 billion, but are in fact $85 billion. If this is the case, that's $270 for every single American every single month ($3238 per American per year). See Don Lee, "Federal Reserve Officials are Split on When to End Stimulus Program," *Los Angeles Times,* July 10, 2013. Accessible at http://www.latimes.com/business/money/la-fi-mo-fed-minutes-20130710,0,1856947.story . Lee writes, "Federal Reserve policymakers appear to be deeply split on how quickly to pull back their $85 billion a month bond-buying stimulus."

family.[72] How free is a country when its people shoulder over $11.31 trillion in consumer debt in the form of home mortgages, home equity lines of credit, auto loans, credit card loans, student loans and other loans[73] and real wages for the bottom 99% of the working population have been flat or declining for at least 30 years?[74]. If we add to household debt the debt of federal, state, and local governments, and financial institutions and other businesses, the total debt that Americans owe is a staggering $58 trillion.[75]

See also Pedro da Costa and Alister Bull, "Fed Split in June on QE timing; Bernanke Sees Easy Policy for Now," Reuters, July 10, 2013. Da Costa and Bull write, "Global investors have recently recovered from a mild bout of panic sparked when Bernanke sketched out the Fed's expectations for ending its bond purchases. The Fed has been buying $85 billion a month in U.S. government and mortgage related debt." We've had a five-year (and seemingly now endless) program to buy the debt of the securitized gambling operations of Wall Street banks—so they can't lose. Only we the people lose—over and over and over again. Accessible at http://www.reuters.com/article/2013/07/10/us-usa-fed-bernanke-idUSBRE9690Y620130710 .

[70] Nomi Prins, *It Takes a Pillage: An Epic Tale of Power, Deceit, and Untold Trillions.* Hoboken: John Wiley and Sons, 2009, updated 2011. See also http://www.nomiprins.com/.

[71] Nomi Prins and Christopher Hayes, "Meet the Hazards," *The Nation,* October 2009. Accessible at http://www.thenation.com/article/meet-hazzards#axzz2WIHG38Vu.

[72] The average American family has a savings of $5,740—maybe enough to live for two months without catastrophic collapse. See www.federalreserve.gov and www.uscensus.gov.

[73] Federal Reserve Bank of New York, 2012 Third Quarter Report on Household Debt and Credit, Consumer Credit Panel/Equifax. Available at http://www.newyorkfed.org/research/national_economy/householdcredit/DistrictReport_Q32012.pdf .

[74] See "Going Nowhere: Worker's Wages Since the Mid-1970s," The Century Foundation, 2008. Available at http://www.tcf.org/assets/downloads/tcf-GoingNowhere.pdf .

See also the National Jobs for All Coalition wage reports at http://www.njfac.org/.

[75] See www.federalreserve.gov.

And every minute that goes by, the problem gets worse, not better, so time serves merely to strengthen my argument. I don't know about you, but my calculator doesn't even get close to having enough digits to enter that number--$58 trillion. $58 trillion in total debt from all sources works out to $184,401 per citizen. This includes children and people who are beyond retirement age, so once again, if we calculated these non-workers out, the argument would only be more conclusive. But I won't do that, because the weakest case—the best case scenario—is still so horrifying that nothing more will need to be said. And before we blow the political trumpet, let's clear the air: this issue is so bipartisan that it's tripartisan, or, I'll go even further: polypartisan, multipartisan, what have you. If you are breathing, you are affected (and, in fact, due to tax laws, even if you are not breathing). Only a few will see it as an issue we don't need to discuss--the same few who continue to benefit immensely from our not discussing it.

But let's get back to the issue at hand: in these United States of America, the "richest country on earth", debt per citizen is $184,401 (Remember that savings per family is $5,740).[76]

If we add all personal assets owned by Americans together (excluding corporate and business), the total is $66.9 trillion. According to the Economic Policy Institute, the top 1% owns 35.6% of

---

See also www.usdebtclock.org.

[76] See www.federalreserve.gov and www.uscensus.gov.

all wealth.[77] This is one of the lowest percentages for the top 1% that you will find and the numbers for this economic group continue to go up consistently, year after year. The Nobel Prize winning economist Joseph E. Stiglitz puts the number at 40%[78] We'll go with lower number here: 35.6%.[79] If we subtract this percentage from $66.9 trillion ($23.81 trillion), we are left with $43.09 trillion in assets shared by the 99%.[80] 99% of the population is 312 million persons. $43.09 trillion divided by 312 million is $138,108 in assets per citizen. If we subtract the debt from all sources per citizen ($184,401), we arrive at a per capita debt of $46,293 for the bottom 99% of the population. If we add back all corporate and business assets at the prorated percentage (64.4% for the bottom 99%, a number that is arguably too high), we have $59.89 trillion in total assets, divided by 312 million, which is $191,961 per capita, minus $184,401 debt per capita which yields a shocking net worth of $7,560 each for the bottom 99%. Now, let's add in savings for the real numbers. The average American family, as noted, has a savings of $5,740. There are 2.6 persons per

---

[77] See Lawrence Mishel, Josh Bivens, Elise Gould, and Heidi Shierholz, *The State of Working America*, 12th edition, Economic Policy Institute, Cornell University Press, 2012. See http://stateofworkingamerica.org/files/book/Chapter6-Wealth.pdf

for numbers on wealth.

[78] Joseph Stiglitz, "Of the 1%, by the 1%, for the 1%," *Vanity Fair,* May 2011. Accessible at http://www.vanityfair.com/society/features/2011/05/top-one-percent-201105.

[79] Obviously, this number cannot include the wealth in secret offshore accounts. 35.6%, therefore, is the percentage of legally known wealth owned by the 1%.

[80] See Economic Policy Institute, "The State of Working America, 2011: Wealth Holdings Remain Unequal in Good and Bad Times." Accessible at http://inequality.org/wealth-inequality/.

household, so the savings per capita is $2,207. When we add the savings per capita, we arrive at a net worth of $9,767 per person for the bottom 99%. Note that the start asset number in this calculation ($191,961) is over 1.5 times the $120,000 stated earlier, as this more optimistic number of $191,961 does not even account for the fact that the vast majority of corporate and business assets are disproportionately owned by the 1%. If you factor in this variable, the bottom 99% of all Americans will arguably show no net worth. Again, we must keep in mind that these are the *reported* numbers, so undisclosed foreign accounts are absent from the above calculations, accounts that one could reasonably speculate belong disproportionately to the same 1% that owns 35.6 – 40.0% of the reported wealth. It is eminently reasonable, then, to conclude that wealth inequity in America is even more extreme, but we'll stick with the stated numbers.

We live in a country that has developed the most efficient system ever devised and that the world has ever seen to peacefully create wealth for and transfer wealth to a small fraction of individuals living within said system. (We may call it peaceful, if we leave out numerous wars of aggression, prolonged exploitation of foreign resources and labor, massive weapon sales, instigation of foreign coups, secret and not-so-secret detention and torture facilities, drone attacks, etc.   See Chapter 7: "It Takes A Killing" for more on this). Unparalleled free market capitalism[81] truly is the American experiment par excellence.[82]

Back to the numbers. The picture is even less rosy if we crunch numbers for the bottom 95% of the population (300 million Americans). The bottom 95% owns 36.5% of total assets, or $24.41 trillion (without corporate and business assets), yielding a net worth of $81,366 per capita.[83] When we subtract the $184,401 debt per capita, we arrive at a per capita debt of $103,034 for the bottom 95% of the population. If we add back all corporate and business assets at the prorated percentage (36.5%), the figure for total assets owned by the bottom 95% is $33.94 trillion, which works out to $113,133 per person. When we subtract the per capita debt of $184,401, we arrive at a per capita debt of $71,267 for the bottom 95% of the population. If we add back the per capita savings of $2,207, we arrive at a final number of $69,060 per capita debt for the bottom 95% of the population. Let me state this again: the bottom 95% of all Americans do not have a net worth. They instead have an average debt of $69,060.

These numbers might reflect something that you

---

[81] A "free market", that is, coupled with a monstrously regressive tax code [See David Kay Johnston, *Perfectly Legal: The Covert Campaign to Rig Our Tax System to Benefit the Super Rich – and Cheat Everyone Else* (New York: Portfolio Trade, 2003, updated 2005)] and publically financed private corporations (in the form of bailouts, tax incentives and impunity from liability). Put differently, one might say that the free market exists only for the 99%, if by "free" we include the stipulation that real and total loss of capital (in the form of money and property) is possible. To the extent that this stipulation does not apply to the 1%, they do not participate in the free market. $17.5 trillion in bailouts (and counting)? If that's free, then freedom is slavery, war is peace and ignorance is strength. See George Orwell, *1984* (New York: Harcourt Brace, 2003), 4.

[82] The province of kings and nobles by another name and unfomenting, always unfomenting revolution.

[83] Economic Policy Institute.

have been feeling for a long, long time. Although Americans are more educated than ever, the overwhelming majority are getting further behind day after day, year after year, in spite of working more jobs and longer hours.[84] According to the Pew Research Center, just during the economic "recovery" of 2009 – 2011, the net wealth of the top 7% grew by a staggering 28%, while the bottom 93% lost 4%.[85]

Forget it, you might say, you're not crunching the numbers right at all. What you're doing is a bunch of voodoo economics.[86] You've got to calculate more specifically, by income group, based on net worth. Okay, let's do that. Well, I tried that too, and it looks like a zero sum game all around. Using the same numbers from the Economic Policy Institute[87], those in the 95.0 – 99.0% percentile (12.6 million), owning 27.9% of the personal wealth, have a total per capita net worth of 1.29 million after subtracting the prorated

---

[84] See the Brookings Institute article written by Michael Greenstone and Adam Looney, directors at the Hamilton Project: "The Great Recession May Be Over, But American Families are Working Harder Than Ever," July 8, 2011. Accessible at http://www.brookings.edu/blogs/jobs/posts/2011/07/08-jobs-greenstone-looney.

[85] Yes, what the corporate media portrays as an economic "recovery" was yet another loss for the bottom 93%. There was no "end" to the "Great Recession" for anyone but the wealthiest segment of our society. See the Pew Research Center study by Richard Fry and Paul Taylor, "A Rise in Wealth for the Wealthy; Declines for the Lower 93%," Pew Research Center, April 23, 2013. Accessible at http://www.pewsocialtrends.org/2013/04/23/a-rise-in-wealth-for-the-wealthydeclines-for-the-lower-93/.

[86] Not that this hasn't been done before—and considered scientific.

[87] See Lawrence Mishel, Josh Bivens, Elise Gould, and Heidi Shierholz, *The State of Working America*, 12th edition, Economic Policy Institute, Cornell University Press, 2012. See http://stateofworkingamerica.org/files/book/Chapter6-Wealth.pdf .

amount of the $58 trillion in debt. Those in the 80.1 – 95.0% percentile, owning 23.7% of the personal wealth, have a total per capita net worth of $151,160. So, we're saying on this analysis that if you make it into the top economic quintile in America but not the top 5%, you may actually own a quarter or half a house, maybe a car or two, and have a few thousand in what's left of your 401K. So if you lose your job in an "economic downturn", you could go for what?--40 days and nights before everything starts crashing down around you?

And what about the other 80% of the population? Those in the bottom 80% of the American population, economically speaking, have a negative net worth of $150,420. Yes, carved up in this way, the bottom 252 million Americans have a negative net worth of over $150,000 per capita. And none of these above numbers include the per capita interest on all debts that comprise the $58 trillion, which is currently running at $10,487 per citizen per year.[88] That's $28.73 in interest every American is paying every single day of the year, on average, on all combined debt. And, once again, these are the numbers that give the bottom 99% the highest discernable share of the wealth, not the even more horrifying numbers from economist Joseph Stiglitz.

But wait, you might say. Something's got to be wrong. Even if your numbers are right, you're pinning them on the wrong people. For example, you continue, that $16.503 trillion that comprises the current Federal debt ($52,345 per citizen) isn't something that's actually owed by each American, no,

---

[88] Bureau of Economic Analysis. See www.bea.gov.

that's not their debt—it's the debt of the Federal government. People don't actually have to pay it back, no, it's just going to be erased over a ten to twenty year period after the Federal budget is balanced. Or, you may argue that when 16.5 trillion dollars worth of handout programs like Social Security and Medicare and Medicaid are cut, then the Federal debt will be eliminated in short order.

Really? To begin with, every American who works any length of time in any given year pays in to Social Security (6.2%; 12.4% if self-employed), Medicare and Medicaid (1.45%; 2.9% if self-employed), so you'd be taking their money to pay down the Federal debt.[89] Even if you don't pay a cent of federal income tax because your income is simply too low, you still pay into Social Security and Medicare. For example, if you earn $10,000, you will pay $765 for Social Security and Medicare (All numbers will be figured as an employee. Double all the numbers for the self-employed).

If you make $20,000, you will pay $1530. If your income is this low (which is not at all uncommon), the amount you pay into these programs can seem like a great deal of money, even a make-or-break proposition. Social Security tax is capped at an income of $110,100, so if you make $20 million a year, your Social Security tax is $6826, the same as the guy making $110,100 a year.

The percentage of Social Security liability for someone making $10,000 a year is 6.2 percent, but if you make

---

[89] Thus, in utilizing this circuitous route to make them pay the bill, you demonstrate that you believe that it is in fact their debt. And clearly, that is what the sequester is all about. Just look at the WhiteHouseSpeak: http://www.whitehouse.gov/issues/sequester.

$20,000,000, your percentage is only .034 percent. The guy making 10K is thus paying 182 times the percentage of Social Security tax as the guy making $20 million. So yes, each American who has an earned income would be paying off the Federal debt–– even if they didn't pay a dime in federal taxes.

If you argue that we can simply transfer the debt to citizens who are not yet in the workforce, I would say yes, we could do that (if the economy doesn't collapse in the meantime), if your solution to the problem of wealth inequity is simply to force the next generations to bear the burden. I can't argue with that as a fiscal solution, if the goal is merely to transfer debt. The means to transfer wealth is a well-developed art both nationally and internationally; and a corollary, an epiphenomenon if you will, of such wealth transfer is the conferral of debt. Conferring debt in a zero-sum-game economy is the necessary corollary of transferring wealth (whereas in a non-zero-sum-game economy, this would not be the case). The debt is conferred, of course, on those who do not possess the wealth to prevent the conferral.

We could ponder a moment to think about the $17.5 trillion in bailout money, mostly done in secret.[90] To whom did that money go? Why did the Federal government transfer $17.5 trillion to a small (indeed very small, far less that 1%) segment of our population, when the net effect (you don't need a PhD

---

[90] See Nomi Prins, *It Takes a Pillage: An Epic Tale of Power, Deceit, and Untold Trillions* (Hoboken: John Wiley and Sons, 2009, updated 2011). See also http://www.nomiprins.com/.

See also Nomi Prins and Christopher Hayes, "Meet the Hazards," *The Nation*, October 2009. Accessible at http://www.thenation.com/article/meet-hazzards#axzz2WlHG38Vu.

in economics to understand this, or even a high school diploma) would be to transfer the debt to the rest of the American people in the form of Federal debt? (If personal debt for the 99% had actually gone down after the trillions in bailout monies were released, possibly someone might credibly argue that some of this money went to these 312 million Americans--the 99%--but since these debts did not go down, this argument cannot plausibly be made). Maybe it even seems odd to you that the bailout numbers ($13.3 to $17.5 billion and rising, with more "quantitative easing" every month, thanks to the Federal Reserve) almost directly mirror the current Federal debt. Oh no, you might say, this series of "injections" of cash "into the economy" (read: pockets of a few) actually creates wealth for all those people who will end up paying off the Federal debt--and these "injections", in the end, create much more wealth than the $17.5 trillion (and counting) transferred. Really? Well, the onus of proof would be on you in that case.[91] I'm sorry to say that I only see the full bailout numbers mirrored in the current Federal debt numbers. And when we add up all the debt numbers, we come back to the fact that the bottom 80% of the American population has an average per capita negative net worth of $150,400. 252 million people who literally have nothing to lose. Just getting back to zero would be somehow... progress. And when it comes to "too big to fail", there's one thing that's certain: whoever is talking

---

[91] We know that this is not the case. All of the wealth—and more—went to the top. Once again, see the Pew Research Center study by Richard Fry and Paul Taylor, "A Rise in Wealth for the Wealthy; Declines for the Lower 93%," Pew Research Center, April 23, 2013. Accessible at http://www.pewsocialtrends.org/2013/04/23/a-rise-in-wealth-for-the-wealthydeclines-for-the-lower-93/.

isn't talking about you.

The average American doesn't have a net worth, unless by net worth we mean negative net worth. Being too small to succeed, you have already failed, if by failing we mean having no net worth and no rational grounds for a belief in a positive outcome for your own personal financial future. And you can see from the numbers above that it doesn't just stop with the average American. The bottom 80% of the population has a negative net worth, and it isn't until you rise to somewhere well north of the 80th percentile (best case scenario above) that you get to those who have no net worth. Put differently, despite ever rising productivity, year after year, 80%+ of our population have absolutely nothing to show for it, since 80%+ have either no net worth or a negative net worth. (If you go with the first series of numbers, the bottom 95% of the population has absolutely no net worth.)   Lest one argue that Americans, the most productive society on the face of the earth, are lazy, we should remember the fact that Americans workers have an astounding record when it comes to productivity, and they are working increasingly longer hours.[92] What do you think? Does it sound like something is wrong with this picture? Or are you too tired from overwork to think about it?

There are two obvious conclusions that can be drawn at this juncture from this economic analysis:

---

[92] See Michael Greenstone and Adam Looney, "The Great Recession May Be Over, But American Families are Working Harder Than Ever," July 8, 2011. Accessible at http://www.brookings.edu/blogs/jobs/posts/2011/07/08-jobs-greenstone-looney.

(1) Resources (assets) are not infinite. Finitude means scarcity. A prognosticatory model predicated on the notion of a constantly expanding economy is nothing short of delusional.   When total assets for all Americans combined are $93 trillion and all nonbusiness assets are $66.9 trillion, and the top 1% has 35.6 – 40.0 percent of those (identifiable) assets, everyone else has got to scramble just to avoid personal economic collapse. To go further: the planet simply does not contain the resources for an international elite to continue to own and control as much as half of all the world's wealth, assets, and power.   Such a situation disenfranchises billions around the globe, rendering them voiceless and invisible.   This is a condition of chronic, systemic violence.

(2) The overwhelming majority of Americans have absolutely nothing to show for all the years and tens of thousands of hours they (and their ancestors) have toiled to make a life for themselves in this great land of promise. If either of the above economic analyses is correct, somewhere between 252 million and 300 million Americans would actually benefit from a total reconstruction of our centralized, tightly (and privately) controlled, wholly monetized economy. To go further: if such a reconstruction is not imminently forthcoming, a "market correction" will take place in accordance with the organic and unwritten laws

governing all struggles for human and civil rights.[93] The current economic structure, anchored in systemic violence, can only maintain its precarious equilibrium for so long.

How free is a country when there have been 16.54 million home foreclosures between the years of 2008 – 2012,[94] not including business, church and other foreclosures?   If we look at the years 2000 – 2012, the number of home foreclosures is a cataclysmic 23,771,253. Let's look at these numbers. Calculating an average of 2.6 residents per dwelling,[95] 61.8 million Americans have lost their homes since 2000. That's 19.6% of our population. 61.8 million people...homeless? Or, we can look at it another way: there were 132.3 million housing units in the United States in 2011, and the home ownership rate was 66.1%[96] Therefore, there were 87.45 million homeowners.   23.77 million foreclosures on homes since 2000 and 16.54 million since 2008? That would be somewhere between 18.9% and 27.2% of all currently owned housing units, and this is just in the last 12 years. And of course, by homeowner we really mean lender-owned home, in all but a very few cases.

---

[93] Cf. Albert Camus, *The Rebel: An Essay on Man in Revolt*, trans.

Anthony Bower (New York: Vintage, 1956).

[94] See Moody's Analytics and RealtyTrac at U.S. foreclosure data at https://www.economy.com/home/products/realtytrac.asp .

See also www.realtytrac.com and www.federalreserve.gov .

[95] See www.census.gov.

[96] See www.census.gov.

Homeownership is part of the American dream?[97] And who—ever—actually owns his or her own home?[98] And then, of course, there are those who actually do own two, three, four homes, and maybe a fifth in Costa Rica. (This fact actually lowers the total number of homeowners, making the statistics that much worse.) One thing you can be sure of: they are not in the bottom 99% of the population.

Oh, and we forgot to talk about the other kind of real estate transaction that has gotten an enormous amount of traction since the ongoing $17.5 trillion transfer of wealth: the short sale (short in name only, in market terms, most take a very, very long time). Most people don't know much at all about the unwieldy beast known as a short sale, even if they are in the midst of one. This type of transaction falls under the "distressed sale" category, since the borrower has gotten behind on payments and instead of a home foreclosure, the bank agrees to allow the "owner" to sell the home for a price that is less than the outstanding loan amount.

---

[97] Recent evidence suggests that in the current economic climate, home ownership might be a liability. For example see Floyd Norris, "Challenge to Dogma on Owning a Home," *New York Times,* May 9, 2013. Accessible at http://www.nytimes.com/2013/05/10/business/homeownership-may-actually-cause-unemployment.html?pagewanted=all&_r=0. Norris' article is based on a recent study by Dartmouth Professor David G. Blanchflower and University of Warwick (England) Professor Andrew J. Oswald, both professors of economics, who argue that home ownership may actually cause unemployment—although the relationship is anything but straightforward, until you think about it. "We find that a high rate of homeownership slowly decimates a labor market," says Oswald. Home ownership, it turns out, creates "negative externalities" for the labor market. Capital wants infinitely malleable labor, available at the beck and call of the corporate master. To the degree that the worker owns anything with any degree of marginal permanence, the worker will be less available for exploitation.

[98] According to the United States Census Bureau, the current rate of homeownership is 65.0%, but once again, this is simply a measure of whose name is on the deed, not whether a bank holds the note on the home. See http://www.census.gov/housing/hvs/files/currenthvspress.pdf.

The lender, of course, would only agree to this if they thought they couldn't do any better, so agreeing to a short sale on the part of the lender means that they're pretty sure they've not only tapped out the borrower but the market as well. Lenders are going so far as to incentivize the short sale process for borrowers by giving them cash
to agree to such an arrangement.[99] The short sale seems to be the latest trend on the part of lending institutions. If we add the short sale numbers to the 23.771 million home foreclosures, the total number of distressed sales and foreclosures is certainly a significant percentage of all current home sales. "Distressed", as a market category, presumes, of course, that homeowners had the intention of actually owning the home at some point, lest their closing costs (inspections, home insurance, mortgage insurance, loan origination fee, document fees, recording fees, prorated real estate taxes, attorney and realtor fees if applicable) and monthly mortgage payments are all for naught. The stress and economic instability caused by a distressed (or rather, coerced) sale all but rule out the possibility that such persons had planned the event as a covert market strategy. Does anyone sign fifteen documents on the dotted line, thinking that the whole thing is going to end in a horrible disaster?

---

[99] See Prashant Gopal, "Banks Paying Homeowners to Avoid Foreclosures," Bloomberg News, February 6, 2012. Accessible at http://www.bloomberg.com/news/2012-02-07/banks-paying-homeowners-a-bonus-to-avoid-foreclosures-mortgages.html.

How free is a country where 1,346,677 people declare personal bankruptcy every year[100] and the number one cause of bankruptcy (62.1% of all filings and climbing) is medical debt?[101] The number of personal bankruptcy filings has increased 473% since 1980, and 95% of all Americans still have more debt than ever, while the elite have more assets than ever. How can one make it out? Does this make sense to you? How would indentured servitude have been worse, especially if there were an actual release date? And 78% of those who declare bankruptcy due to health care costs actually have health insurance?

---

[100] This is the average of the last four reported years, 2008 – 2011. See the American Bankruptcy Institute statistics at www.abiworld.org.

[101] See David U. Himmelstein, MD, Deborah Thorne, Ph.D., Elizabeth Warren, JD, and Steffie Woolhandler, MD, MPH, "Medical Bankruptcy in the United States," *The American Journal of Medicine,* 2009. The results: " Using a conservative definition, 62.1% of all bankruptcies in 2007 were medical…Most medical debtors were well educated, owned homes, and had middle-class occupations. Three quarters had health insurance." Conclusion: "Illness and medical bills contribute to a large and increasing share of US bankruptcies." (2). This study actually notes that 78% of those who declare bankruptcy for medical reasons had health insurance…at the start of the illness(s). This is a sad commentary for any civilization.

See also Colorado Public Radio and Erika Gonzalez, "Patients Go Bankrupt As Medical Costs Soar," May 21, 2012. Accessible at http://www.kunc.org/post/patients-go-bankrupt-medical-costs-soar#.UcuirbkUnR8.email .

See also Joan Brunwasser, "Harvard Study: Personal Bankruptcies Not Controlled by Mass. Health Plan," Physicians for A National Health Program, March 8, 2011. Accessible at http://www.pnhp.org/news/2011/march/harvard-study-personal-medical-bankruptcies-not-controlled-by-mass-health-plan .

See also Tara Parker-Pope, "Medical Bills Cause Most Bankruptcies," *New York Times,* June 4, 2009. Accessible at http://well.blogs.nytimes.com/2009/06/04/medical-bills-cause-most-bankruptcies/?emc=eta1 .

Finally, see Catherine Arnst, "Study Links Medical Costs and Personal Bankruptcy," *Bloomberg Business Week,* June 4, 2009. Accessible at http://www.businessweek.com/bwdaily/dnflash/content/jun2009/db2009064_6 66715.htm#rshare=email_article .

Doesn't this sound like some kind of a cruel joke?

How free is a country in which 48.6 million persons do not have any type of health insurance, and as many million are underinsured?[102] (Or more. This type of statistic is hard to come by, being partially subjective). And many of those who have insurance struggle to pay the premiums and yet cannot guarantee that a claim will not be denied?[103] In 2013, 48.6 million do not have health insurance coverage, up 12 million from 2000, when the number of uninsured was 36.6 million. Federal health care reform has lowered the number from 49.9 million to 48.6 million, mainly due to the fact that those aged 22 – 26 are now able to remain on their parent's insurance. Under the guise of real health care reform, for-profit health insurance corporations have induced a beholden Congress to pass legislation that will ensure,

---

[102] Not that it matters, given what we've noted above. Health insurance provides no guarantee against medical bankruptcy. But we'll continue for the sake of argument.

[103] See Brett O'Hara and Kyle Caswell, "Health Status, Health Insurance, and Medical Services Utilization: 2010," United States Census Bureau, October 2012. Accessible at http://www.census.gov/prod/2012pubs/p70-133.pdf.

See also Carmen DeNavas-Walt, Bernadette D. Proctor and Jessica C. Smith, "Income, Poverty, and Health Insurance Coverage in the United States: 2011," United States Census Bureau, September 2012. Accessible at http://www.census.gov/prod/2012pubs/p60-243.pdf.

As we have already seen, health insurance is no guarantee of security when it comes to injury or illness. What we really need access to isn't health *insurance* but health *care*, especially given the fact that there seems to be little or no intersection between the two. A future study may indicate that health insurance is actually a contributory factor in medical bankruptcy, as people struggle to pay exorbitant and ever increasing premiums. There is no need to demonstrate the fact that many Americans have paid tens of thousands in health insurance premiums, some even six figures (and this, even if they are "well"). A contributory factor in bankruptcy? How could it be otherwise? A contributory factor in medical bankruptcy? Again, how could it be otherwise?

for these same corporations, millions of new "customers" from whom they can extract profit, through claim denial and exorbitant and ever-increasing premiums, to transfer to their shareholders, executives and owners (the vast majority of whom are at the top of the economic ladder); and if these prospective customers are too "poor" to pay the full premiums for such coverage, the government will supplement their contributions and make direct payments to these for-profit health insurance corporations. 48.6 million Americans have already decided that even though this is literally a matter of life and death, they are not in a position to purchase for-profit health insurance. How could anyone make such a decision lightly? And the best we can do as a society is issue a government mandate to all citizens to participate in the for-profit health insurance industry or else the government will do it for you, with your money? (Or with money you will effectively be forced to borrow. All money spent by those in the bottom 80%+ is effectively borrowed money.) Is this what we call a civilization? A civilization for whom?

What about food and nutrition? How free is country in which 46.8 million citizens (14.5 – 14.9%), most of them children, are food insecure, meaning that they lack adequate calories/nutrition to provide for sound human health?[104]

---

[104] See "Household Food Security in the United States 2011," United States Department of Agriculture Economic Research Service. The USDA reported that in 2011, 17.6 million American households (14.9%) were food insecure. Accessible at http://www.ers.usda.gov/publications/err-economic-research-report/err141.aspx#.Ucum7fYFQyM.email .

See also the world and United States hunger data from the World Hunger Education Service at http://www.worldhunger.org/articles/Learn/us_hunger_facts.htm .

When it comes to poverty, the situation is no better. The fact is that according to the United States Census, 46.2 million Americans (15.0%) live in poverty, a number that is going in the wrong direction.[105]

The reality of the economic situation, according to veteran consumer advocate and writer Ralph Nader, is that the United States is "an advanced Third-World country". Our government, Nader maintains, is now controlled by big business. The United States has succumbed to a system that is, to use Nader's phrase, "American fascism."[106]

See also data from FeedingAmerica.org, "Hunger Statistics, Hunger Facts and Poverty Facts" at http://feedingamerica.org/hunger-in-america/hunger-facts/hunger-and-poverty-statistics.aspx . The data present a compelling indictment of a failed social policy.

Finally, see the CNN report "Nearly 15 Percent of Americans Face 'Food Insecurity,'" *CNN*, November 16, 2010. Accessible at http://eatocracy.cnn.com/2010/11/16/nearly-15-percent-of-americans-face-food-insecurity/ .

[105] See Karen Weise, "Record U.S. Poverty Rate Holds As Inequality Grows," *Bloomberg Business Week*, September 12, 2012. Accessible at http://www.businessweek.com/articles/2012-09-12/record-u-dot-s-dot-poverty-rate-holds-as-inequality-grows . Even the Wall Street titans can see that the zero sum game is rigged—and that pointing it out won't change a thing (thus, they can certainly point it out). The corporate analysis of this same data, of course, requires suspension of disbelief.

[106] Ralph Nader, *Democracy Now* interview with Amy Goodman and Aaron Mate, June 4, 2013. Accessible at http://www.democracynow.org/blog/2013/6/4/ralph_nader_on_the_federal_res erves_gamble_bradley_manning_fighting_the_two_party_system.

The concept of fascism here invoked is not inaccurate if one interprets the Italian from which it is derived—*fascismo,* from *fascio*—"bundle" or "political group". A small bundle or political group controls the destiny of the nation. In this case, it is the oligarchs and plutocrats, those that through their massive wealth (which is antithetical to a democratic society) dictate the aims and means of the state.

So much for even the last vestiges and pretense of democracy.

* * * * *

The international elite are neither Christian nor Jewish, neither Muslim nor Hindu, neither Buddhist nor Sikh. No, they are above all that. They worship at a more "elemental" altar, the animate worshipping the inanimate. If they exhibited so much as a meager propensity for metaphysics, our planet wouldn't be what it is today, and our children wouldn't live in a world with a future so uncertain that rational prognosticators are dubious concerning whether there will be a future at all, at least for Homo sapiens.

No, the international elite are clearly above any metaphysical considerations regarding the world around them, be they animate or inanimate. They are immune to considerations of respect, awe, reverence, duty, openness, stewardship, empathy or justice. Whatever else they are or may be, they have worked to imbue world civilization with a thoroughgoing materialism as they have spread the utilitarian gospel of monetization and exploitation. They have sought to create the world in their image––a soulless place of parasitic hopelessness, distrust, and decay.

The international elite are, above all, materialists––truly a religion of unparalleled addictiveness. They cast their nets to spread their gospel, to entice through their only charms (money, power and self-designated glamour) the poor, the meek, the disenfranchised, to accept their deadly gifts, to silence the spirit with mammon, to stanch the wound with things that hold no lasting value, that serve to mask, momentarily, the hopelessness and bankruptcy of the new and at the same time most ancient religion. They seek to mask the resultant and ever-growing universal despair with an endless barrage of cheap, ephemeral material "goods" made by de facto slaves––flat screen plasma HD TVs, smart phones, tablet computers, electronic readers, GPS devices, video games, and so much more.

There is no doubt that materialism may appear progressive, beautiful, rational, enlightened. But alas, these are but appearances, hiding a reality that is not amenable to advertising spin or market calculation or political machination, a reality that dictates to us what we must do if we desire to live beyond a brief moment upon planet earth. Maybe that is not meant to be. But if not, in the meantime we are still at liberty to face the end as something other than materialists. We are still at liberty to face the end with respect, awe, empathy, and contrition. We can begin by facing the end today. Does it portend our imminent demise? Or a new renaissance? Have we been living with the delusion that what we do somehow does not matter, does not make a difference, is not meaningful?

Think about it. We are not going to be rescued from on high. Informed, self-reflective, intelligent, empathic, self-respecting and courageous action is the only path we can take––a path yet to be carved from the material jungle––in order to create a world in which we will, in the end, want to live. That is, if living is really what we want to do.

CHAPTER NINE

WHAT IS PHILOSOPHY AND WHY DOES ANYBODY CARE?

Philosophy is a discipline heard of by all and understood by (almost) none. Maybe nobody has a clue. Even Socrates didn't claim to know anything about philosophy: "All that I know is that I know nothing"--which doesn't sound like he knows much about philosophy, let alone anything else.[107] What the heck is it all about? And what good does philosophy do us mere mortals on this hurtling sphere?

Philosophy is an ancient discipline, beginning essentially with the written word itself. Or, one might say, before the written word.[108]

---

[107] Plato, *Apology,* as found in Plato, *Five Dialogues: Euthyphro, Apology, Crito, Meno, Phaedo,* trans. G.M.A. Grube (Indianapolis: Hackett, 1981), 23-44. In fact, this famous phrase assigned to Socrates doesn't actually appear in Plato's writings, and since Socrates didn't write anything (as far as we know), all we can do is look at what Plato put into the mouth of Socrates in the *Apology,* a dialogue that recounts the trial and ultimate conviction of Socrates in 399 BCE. Upon conviction, he is given the death sentence. What Socrates essentially argues in the *Apology* is that it is better to know you don't know something than to think you know something that you don't know (See, e.g. p. 34 [Section 29]). Subsequently Socrates, in famous Socratic fashion, continues to enumerate things about which he claims to know nothing. The one thing that Socrates does claim to know, the one thing about which Socrates is certain, is that it has "been enjoined upon me by the god" to be a philosopher (p. 37 [Section 33]). Socrates makes it clear that he believes that "the god ordered me...to live the life of a philosopher (p.34 [Section 28, 29]).

[108] Possibly even before the spoken word. If thought requires language, philosophy is coextensive with both thought and language. If thought does not require language, philosophy predates even language.

It begins with human beings in their insatiable quest to understand themselves and their world.

Philosophy is an attempt to make (rational) sense of ourselves and the world in which we live.[109]

Philosophy, one might say (and in fact, I am saying it here) is the bastard child of theology. First, we have theo-ology, or the study of God, the gods, the immaterial (which, after all, is a dramatically difficult thing to study). For what can we say about that which is immaterial, that which is beyond science, that which is beyond sense perception? Some were not satisfied with the answers supplied by the theologians or doctors of religion, those who were supposed to know about the things beyond this mortal sphere. Those who could not accept the standard answers--we could call them skeptics, or philosophers--had to look elsewhere for the truth about themselves and the nature of the cosmos. Such skeptics sought answers without appealing to revelation, myth, holy writ, tradition, superstition, or authority. They decided that they wanted to figure it out for themselves. They decided they needed to know if it was even possible to figure it out for themselves--and if not, the quest still had value in itself. They were the philosophers: lovers of wisdom. For such men and women, to really know something was to understand it for themselves, rather than to accept the traditional wisdom or common opinion. And even a self-generated misunderstanding or incomprehension could still hold honor and dignity, as compared to an incurious, obsequious bowing to the wisdom of authority.

---

[109] What counts as rationality is itself a matter of much debate, and sense making may have little to do with rationality. If it does not, we have yet another frontier to explore.

Even a true answer is not true for a philosopher who hasn't derived that truth as a function of his or her own personal journey--a journey fraught with the dangers of madness, loneliness, even death.

Philosophy as a discipline is often traced back to ancient Greece, to Thales, Anaximander, Anaxagoras, Parmenides, Zeno, Heraclitus and of course Socrates, Plato and Aristotle, all living, roughly, between six hundred and three hundred years before the time of Jesus. The Greek philosophers brought reason into the sphere of metaphysics: they wanted to do more than just believe. They wanted to know. Philosophers continue this same quest today. Is it more than simply tilting at windmills? Or hubris (excessive pridefulness) in itself? Does seeking to answer the forever answerless questions have meaning, value, validity in itself?[110]

*   *   *   *   *

Traditionally, philosophy is said to have five "branches" on its most ancient tree. They are:

(1)*Epistemology* – The study of what counts as knowledge. When you say you know something, how is this different from mere belief, if it is different? How do you know that you know anything at all? Are there some things you know that you can't know (whether God exists, for

---

[110] Just because a question appears unanswerable to us as human beings does not, of course, mean that the question does not have an answer. Even if we haven't (or can't) determine the ultimate origin of the cosmos, or whether or not there is a God(s), or whether we have immortal souls does not mean that these questions do not have answers, for it is clear that they do. The cosmos has an ultimate origin, there either are or are not God(s), and we either do or do not have immortal souls.

example), so you have to believe rather than know?

(2) *Metaphysics* – The study of that which is beyond the physical world: Do humans have souls? Is there an afterlife? Does life have a meaning? Is love real? Is there a God? The realm of metaphysics is what traditionally would be known as the "spiritual realm", the realm beyond matter--if there is such a realm. Of course, the epistemological question here is: how do we know that there is a realm beyond the physical world?

(3) *Ethics* – The study of morality. What is the right thing for me to do? Is there a morally correct way to live? Is there a moral law instantiated in the universe? Or do we just make it up as we go along? The philosophical study of ethics seeks not only (usually universal) moral norms and principles but also attempts to prove why they are correct. As always, the philosopher seeks to go beyond mere opinion to the realm of truth-- and to do this, the philosopher must provide evidence that the moral principles, axioms, maxims, etc. are actually valid, true, correct, moral. Another tall order.

(4) *Social and Political Philosophy* – What is the best (most just, equitable) way to organize society? What is the best way to organize social institutions (for example, corporations, schools). Some possible questions: Is it possible to have a

functioning, equitable classless society? Or a society without a government? What are, in fact, the only necessary functions of government, if government is a necessity? If people are basically self-interested (or, evil), must they be threatened or forced to comply with social norms, or will people comply voluntarily without terror and fear?[111] And: Should corporations (insofar as the law is concerned) be considered people? What is freedom of speech? Do human rights exist? If so, what is the origin of human rights? What, in fact, are these rights, if they exist?

(5) *Logic* – Rational analysis of all of the above – and more. Are logical consistency and rationality the same thing? A question for philosophers. This branch of philosophy essentially attempts to discern the appropriate "rules" for reasoning, so that when one presents an "argument" for something, they are presenting the argument in

---

[111] This question separates the strain of political theorists who argue that since humans are basically good, they don't need to be terrorized into social compliance (Locke, Rousseau, Mill, Marx, Sartre) from the strain of theorists who argue that terror and brute force are necessary to ensure compliance with social norms, since humans are basically evil (Machiavelli, Hobbes, Schopenhauer, Freud). Of course, internalized guilt can serve well to regulate behavior, even in the absence of an overwhelming external power. For example, the corporate press argues that a homeowner who is underwater on his or her mortgage should not walk away from his/her mortgage, on the grounds of "moral hazard", yet no one in this same press cries "moral hazard" when illegally and unethically "robosigned" mortgage documents lead to the repossession of the homes of millions of Americans. If the elite class could succeed in inculcating such clear rubbish (the unilateral moral hazard argument, applying it only to the debtor) into the superego of the masses (something they have very nearly completed), the result will be a compliant, docile citizen, a herd animal, a citizen that need not be imprisoned without arrest, tortured, surveilled, or killed by the government in order to maintain the status quo (i.e. protect the interests of the elite). The version of social and political infrastructure that one adopts is, to a large extent, merely an epiphenomenon of one's view of human nature (and one's belief in the malleability of that nature).

a way that can be understood and assessed by others (implying a belief in a certain universality in reason and thought). In this sense, the form of a logical argument transcends any natural language, just as the sonic medium of music transcends any cultural and theoretical conception of music. Can something be true and not true at the same time? Or does this violate a logical principle? Or does it depend upon the "something" in question? Is logic itself merely a deconstructible class construct?

As you can see, we've got a lot to think about. Every thought has not been thought. There is still a vast frontier. There is an illimitable universe of potential thought, an infinitude of as yet incalculable realities. Let's get right to it.

CHAPTER TEN

ON READING PHILOSOPHICAL TEXTS

Philosophical readings are often difficult. Have patience with yourself and give yourself the time to reread the text. Very few people can get it right the first time, so expect to go back over the readings and think through what is being presented.

In particular, make sure that you know first WHAT the writer is trying to prove (the THESIS), and secondly, HOW the writer is proving (or failing to prove) the thesis. If you really understand what is being said, you should be able to restate it in your own words and then be able to find strengths or weaknesses in the argument being presented.

An important thing to remember is that just because the writer says that he or she has proven something doesn't mean that they in fact have proven something. If you're not convinced by what they have to say, you may have very valid objections, so work through finding out just what your objections are (and whether you've got legitimate grounds for your objections).

The final step in thinking things through is developing YOUR OWN position on the issue at hand. This includes being able to give a clear statement of your position and a sequential argument defending that position--something that someone who does not agree with you may look at and follow, even if they do not ultimately agree with you.

To do this, you will need a working knowledge of the relevant facts, since proving something in a vacuum usually translates badly in the real world.

For example, if you are dealing with the issue of gun control you may need to know some relevant facts: do more guns in a society equal a higher or lower body count? That is, do guns really make us safer? Without the relevant facts, your argument is inevitably reduced to an ideological polemic, no matter how passionate, articulate, and founded upon principle. On the other hand, with the relevant facts and a well-argued case, your clearly articulated position may serve to convince someone who had not previously agreed with you. Sometimes, a good philosophical argument--believe it or not--can lead to a change of heart and mind!

CHAPTER ELEVEN

ON THE NATURE AND EXISTENCE OF GOD

Why does the universe exist? Why are we here? Why are you here? Does God exist? Why do we ask these questions in the first place? Is there any way to answer them? Philosophers have asked (and attempted to answer) these questions for thousands of years. These are metaphysical questions that go beyond the boundaries of empirical science. Even if we have no hope of answering such questions with certitude, people will continue to ask them and ponder. Such is the nature of the human being. What does this tell us about ourselves? Our universe?

Anselm (1033 – 1109) attempted to prove that God must exist--based upon a specific conception of God (This is referred to as the "ontological argument").[112] Anselm's proof may well be the most famous proof for God's existence in the history of Western philosophy. How does he do it? Is he cheating somehow, or has he unlocked the secret of the metaphysical universe?

---

[112] Anselm, *Proslogion.* See the Stanford Encyclopedia of Philosophy entry at http://plato.stanford.edu/entries/ontological-arguments/ . This is a fantastic free encyclopedia of philosophy, replete with both primary and secondary source material.

St. Thomas Aquinas (1225-1274) goes further in his five proofs for God's existence, including ontological, cosmological, and teleological demonstrations.[113] This brings us back to an even more basic question: is it even possible to prove that a God or Gods exist? If you say no--how do you know? This claim in itself (that one can never prove that God exists) asserts a certain kind of knowledge (an epistemological claim) about what we can't know. One may even go so far as to argue that agnosticism (claiming that one doesn't or can't know enough to know if God exists) is a knowledge claim in itself that is subject to scrutiny: how can you know enough to know that you can't know enough? If you are only claiming that you don't know enough, the problem could reside within you rather than the universe. Possibly, you could know if only you engaged in further investigation, right?   As with any real philosophical issue, the more you think about it, the more complex it seems.

Is the presence of real evil in the universe (both natural and moral) an argument against the existence of God? If so, how? Or, is the presence of real evil in the universe an argument for the existence of God? The evidence can only be weighed in light of a specific philosophical theory--as is the case with all evidence. Do we live in a moral universe--where some things are right and some wrong--or do we make up our own morality as we go along? Does belief in a supreme being actually affect human behavior? If so, does such belief improve human behavior? Or is the jury still out? Or, does belief in God induce people to act with

---

[113] See Thomas Aquinas, *Summa Theologica*, 1st Part, Question 2 and following. Available at Project Gutenberg's free book project at www.gutenberg.org .

imagined impunity, making the world even worse? Or both? If so, what makes the difference?

One thing seems certain: civilizations today, on the whole, seem just as interested in and preoccupied with questions concerning God and theology as civilizations of antiquity. Does this tell us anything about the nature of the human person and the cosmos in which we find ourselves? A question for philosophers. That, fearless reader, would be you.

CHAPTER TWELVE

EPISTEMOLOGY: WHAT DO I KNOW?

What is the difference between believing and knowing? How do we know that there is a difference? Maybe it's just a matter of belief? If beliefs can be false and can be based upon insufficient evidence, couldn't the same be said about what we think we know (only we don't necessarily know it)? For example, before Copernicus and Galileo, it was considered common knowledge that the sun revolved around the earth. The heliocentric view of the universe, with the sun at the center, was considered by almost everyone to be not only ridiculous, but blasphemous as well. As it turns out, this ridiculous, blasphemous theory was in fact "true" ––or, at least true by current scientific standards.

Another, more recent example: not long ago (even I can remember it), exercise physiologists were telling the world (as was the International Olympic Committee) that women were by nature unfit to compete in many athletic events, that they would sustain permanent damage were they foolish enough to try to compete in many of the more arduous sports (so they were of course prevented from trying). We now know that this is patent nonsense, and women today compete at world-class levels in a myriad of very difficult sports (like marathon running, ultra marathon running and the triathlon). Thousands of examples of this same phenomenon could be given-- what was once considered true (knowledge) has now been discredited.

Have you personally experienced such a phenomenon where what you once thought was obviously true (or false) turned out rather differently than you had imagined? What was it that "woke you up", so to speak? The dilemma is parallel to a situation in which you are actually asleep: if you are actually asleep, can you will yourself awake? If you are cognitively and epistemologically asleep, can you will yourself awake? The question is moot--until you realize that you are actually asleep. Once that happens--if it does happen--you will at that time see the existential choices that lie before you, one of which may entail the attempt to resume your slumber.

CHAPTER THIRTEEN

WHAT IS LOVE?

What is love? Is it possible to live a life without love? Is a life without love worth living? Or is it love that makes life worth living? Does love come from a divine source, or is it simply a trick of biochemistry? Or both? Or something else altogether? Some say "you'll know it when you feel it", but many are deceived by what started out as the "best thing that ever happened" to them. When this happens, it is often very hard to trust yourself--or anybody else--ever again.

Is love an emotion? Or more than an emotion? What does loving reveal about the lover? What we love may tell us more about ourselves than any other single human behavior. It may reveal our desires, aspirations, values, beliefs, hopes and dreams. It may show the lengths to which we will go if we really want something. It certainly will reveal our character, whether the love relationship involves a boyfriend, girlfriend, spouse, or even a family member, friend, or co-worker.

Is your idea of "love" all about how you feel? Is your idea of "love" all about what suits you and makes you happy? Is your idea of "love" all about your own lifestyle of comfort and convenience, prestige and wealth? If it's all about you, how could this really be love, unless we are merely talking about self-love (if we could even call it that)? Sometimes, we may think that because we are "walking on air" and feel better than we have ever felt before that we must be "in love"––but even here the criteria is all about how we feel, not about whether or not we actually have the ability to perceive the other for who he/she is, and accept and care for him/her in a real, concrete way. When it's all about you, it's not love. When it's all about you and you think it's love, it's self-deception. The real question for all of us is how to get beyond narcissism and self-deception to the most important experience a human being is capable of having––a love relationship.

CHAPTER FOURTEEN

PSALM 151: IMPRECATORY

Woe unto you, Corporate CEOs and bankers, hypocrites! For ye shut up the kingdom of earth against the children of men: for ye alone go in yourselves and suffer not those who are not you to enter.[114]

Aceldama.[115] *Woe, woe*.

Woe unto you, Money Lenders and Money Changers, hypocrites and baby killers! For ye devour widow's houses and the houses of the poor and the houses of the handicapped and the houses of the black, brown, yellow, red, and white, and the houses of the desperate, and the houses of United States military personnel, and the houses of the elderly, and the houses of those who have lost their jobs due to mysterious market forces in a global slave labor economy, and for a pretense make long self-serving speeches to Congress and the beholden media and the

---

[114] Cf. Matthew 23:13. King James biblical language will be utilized throughout PSALM 151: IMPRECATORY.

[115] From the Aramaic, *hagel dama* (Greek: *Akeldama*). Literally, *field of blood*: the land purchased by Judas with the bribe money he took for betraying Jesus. See Acts 1:18 – 19.

people of America and the people of the world and those that you are about to crush and those who have to listen to your rationalizations concerning why they must be crushed, if they even warrant a mention, which they usually don't: therefore ye shall receive the greater damnation.[116]

Your seed will be wiped off the face of the earth, just like the international corporate monoliths and their genetically modified seed will wipe all the non-genetically modified seed off the face of the earth.

Aceldama. Woe, woe.

Woe unto you, Corporate Health Insurance Executives and Pharmaceutical Executives, hypocrites! For ye compass sea and land to make one person well, and when she is made, you make her twofold more the child of hell than you are yourselves.[117] Through your exorbitant costs and nefarious stalling tactics, you have successfully genocided those who shall inherit the earth. Push your corpulent bodies up to your fat tables, overflowing with victuals stolen from your silent victims. They will not weep a tear. Continue to stuff yourselves sick behind your gated and walled communities, taking your various potions for overindulgence and indigestion, while turning an endlessly deaf ear to the dying. Take heed, your time is a beggar in the night.

Aceldama. Woe, woe.

Woe unto you, ye blind guides, which say, Whoever shall swear by the poor, the sick, the unemployed, the weak, the broken, the child, the lost, it is nothing; but whosoever shall swear by the gold and the currency

---

[116] Cf. Matthew 23:14.

[117] Cf. Matthew 23:15.

and the stocks and the bonds and the Collateralized Debt Obligations and the Credit Default Swaps and the Inscrutable Derivatives of all Kinds, he is a debtor![118]

You have sold the poor for a pair of shoes,[119] a pair that you have no interest in wearing. They too, must be destroyed, lest you be reminded of that which is no more. Be wary, for you cannot bury them deep enough, their voices will cry from the four winds and drive you to madness. Alas, it is too late! The madness is upon us, has been upon us, will be upon us. But not everlastingly. You will be smitten from the face of the earth and will be remembered no more. This very verse will have no signification, as your memory will be obliterated, along with your heartless deeds.

Aceldama. Woe, woe.

Ye fools and blind: for whether is greater, a simulacra of value, or that for which the simulacra was constructed?[120] Yet you perjure and slander and covet and bear false witness and envy and are filled with grave jealousy, all for the simulacra? When will you recognize the delusion that is your reality? Too late will you realize, and the reaper will be upon you. You will be crushed as a mortar and pestle grind a thing to dust, and then you will be blown as chaff upon a wind of recompense. Do not still your spectral voice of pining. Yet your voice does not pine for them that have not, but for them that have a surfeit and want more and more and more until the mass of your accu-

---

[118] Cf. Matthew 23:16.

[119] Cf. Amos 2:6.

[120] Cf. Matthew 23:17.

mulated existence crushes you beneath its heinous weight. The pointing of your finger of wickedness can only be a self-accusation.

And, Whosoever shall swear by the altar of justice, truth, peace and equity, it is nothing, since anything that is not you or your reflection is nothing; but whosoever sweareth by the gift that is upon it, he is guilty, since the simulacra is to you your own untouchable domain, hence any other who partakes is sure to be charged and never acquitted, but slain first in spirit and then in body.[121] Such is the irremediable nature of your stranglehold on the simulacra. And since you have monetized the universe, the stranglehold is yours and yours alone. Blind guides! It is too late to see; it will always be too late to see. *Aceldama. Woe, woe.*

Ye fools and blind: for whether is greater, the gift of the simulacra that you bestow upon yourselves and yourselves alone, or the altar of human rights, freedom for all creatures great and small, and the dignity of self-governance and self-determination by all that sanctifieth the gift?[122] For ye bloated live as if this were the only world, which, for you, turns out to be the case. For the next will hardly be your world, and we will not so much as dip the tips of our fingers into the cool water so as to slavishly slake your thirst.[123] Ye will thirst for evermore, but not for truth and justice. When these are meted out, your thirst will not for that reason be any more assuaged. Ye will

---

[121] Cf. Matthew 23:18.

[122] Cf. Matthew 23:19.

[123] Cf. Luke 16:19-31.

thirst forever in the presence of the fountain of life, for it is this you have chosen.

Aceldama. Woe, woe.

Whoso therefore shall swear by the altar, sweareth by it, and by all things thereon: truth, justice, righteousness, peace, love; and in so swearing, your false witness will reign down imprecations upon your own selves with your very own slippery, silvery tongues.[124] Ye will resort to the only truth you know: lie. It will not go well with you and your household.

Aceldama. Woe, woe.

And whoso shall swear by the temple, sweareth by it, and by him that dwelleth therein.[125] For your perjured economic forecasts and prognostications, for your self-serving and pernicious expert financial testimony, for your litany of false witnesses in regards to the soundness of our––read: your––economy, you have awakened a giant, a beast that now cannot sleep until such time that you have been recompensed. The Leviathan does not belabor with endless dialogue a false witness. What would be the point? The Leviathan does not hold such as prisoners, knowing the future. Remediation is a possibility of the past and as such, no longer a possibility. For your possibilities have been self-expunged, throttled into one black gauntlet of categorical necessity. Ye have been warned without ceasing, yet ye rail against such warnings as the fearmongering of the ignorant rabble. Even now, it does not occur to you to seek the truth; it is too foreign to your nature. Sleep well, and in your somnambulistic slumber dream of the simulacra you

---

[124] Cf. Matthew 23:20.

[125] Cf. Matthew 23:21.

have created to dominate the world.   There will be a time when such will be taken away from you, even in your dreams. At such time, even a drug-induced sleep will no longer be possible, and your private jet can only take you so far away from the carnage. Never a denizen of your city, Albert Camus spoke to you as you turned a deaf ear: wealth is not acquittal, but merely reprieve.[126] This may no longer ring true, as reprieve will soon be a fading memory. Alas, even the memory is no more.

Aceldama. Woe, woe.

And she that shall swear by heaven, sweareth by the throne of God, and by him that sitteth thereon.[127] For how can you not blaspheme Him who you have not seen, when you without respite blaspheme him who you have seen?[128] You blaspheme when you take from him the little that he needs to sustain human life and dignity, and you blaspheme again when you deny he needs it to live with dignity, or when you blame him for its absence after you have taken it away from him, or when you merely stop your ears and laugh as you shovel another fat serving into your ungrateful and blasphemous gullet.   Why is more than enough not ever enough for you?

Aceldama. Woe, woe.

Woe unto you, Lawyers and Hedge Fund Managers, hypocrites! For ye pay tithes of obeisance to the idols of your own creation, complex synthetic investment

---

[126] Albert Camus, *The Fall,* trans. Justin O'Brien (New York: Vintage, 1991), 82.

[127] Cf. Matthew 23:22.

[128] Cf. I John 4:20.

vehicles, economic cluster bombs, economic nerve gas, economic atomic weapons, economic hydrogen bombs, and have omitted the weightier matters of the law, judgment, mercy, faith, distributive justice, truth and reconciliation, human rights, natural moral law: these ought ye to have done, and to have left the other undone.[129] For when ye poisoned the well of the weak, ye imagined everlasting fresh water for yourselves. Alas, neither fresh water nor everlasting water shall be yours, but only the seductive water of your own poisoning. For evermore.

Aceldama. Woe, woe.

Ye blind guides, which strain at a gnat, and swallow a camel.[130] Ye swallow the camel of opulence while devising machinations to extract crumbs from the poor, saying to yourself, "Why should they have them, if I can take them?" indicating clearly that your right to stolen crumbs is no more than a jest, and power is the only chime you hear. Yet the chimes of freedom resound mightily in the spirit of the oppressed, the weak, the poor, those whose crumbs are being taken by the hand of the dark hunter.[131] Ye know not the day or the hour of your horror, when you will pray that you had never been born.[132] Alas! It will be too late. It will always be too late, since the chime you hear will never alert you to the coming apocalypse. Continue to feast on your carrion and build your bigger and bigger

---

[129] Cf. Matthew 23:23.

[130] Cf. Matthew 23:24.

[131] Cf. Bob Dylan, "Chimes of Freedom" (1964).

[132] Cf. Matthew 25:13.

barns.[133] You are free to choose. But only until you are not. Only until you are not. Until you are not. You are not.

Aceldama. Woe, woe.

Woe unto you, Stockbrokers and Bought Off Politicians, hypocrites! For ye make clean the outside of the cup and of the platter, but within they are full of extortion and excess.[134] For you peddle your platters of CDOs and CDSs and other toxic assets, clean and shiny with hope for the investor: school boards and small municipalities backed into a corner by your merciless stranglehold on world markets and your gutting of any hope for a real tax base. The cup that you peddle seemingly runneth over, but only for a time.[135] As neurotoxins may take time, so it is with econotoxins. Through violence, intimidation, abuse of authority you extort the meager means of the disenfranchised, and so grow to obscene proportions. If your depraved scheme somehow does not net all you were dreaming for and more, ample remains for you to extort the rest from your lackey politicians. You fill the throats of the outraged with your excrement, and so silence them forever.

Aceldama. Woe, woe.

Thou blind Fund Managers, cleanse first that which is within the cup and platter, that the outside of them may be clean also.[136] Clean first the malice afore-

---

[133] Cf. Luke 12:16-24.

[134] Cf. Matthew 23:25.

[135] Cf. Psalm 23:5.

[136] Matthew 23:26.

thought that conjured the toxic assets into being: for they exist as the absence of being. This being is the privation of being: pure evil since Augustine, since the beginning of time.[137]   Cleanse first the greed that created the deaths of millions. Cleanse first the hubris that made you believe that you were the Masters of The Material World, the Big Daddies Suckin' Endlessly at the Trough and, as such, beyond natural and moral law. The blood of the innocents, shed by you, cries out for atonement. The toxicity that you have created flows from the toxicity that is your heart.   Its indelibility is apparent to all save you.

Aceldama. Woe, woe.

Woe unto you, World Bank Swindlers and International Monetary Fund Bloodletters! For ye are like unto whited sepulchers, which indeed appear beautiful outward, but are within full of dead men's bones, and of all uncleanness.[138] For the monies you lend to build a nation are but a ruse so that you may break the backs of all who dwell therein, to bend their necks to your yoke,[139] to sell them down the river, to gut their souls for your miserable mammon.   For your mammonism is global, your tentacles illimitable. Yet your craven soul is shriveled.   Soon the desiccation will turn to petrification and you will breathe no more. It is written in the firmament, to be read by those with eyes to see.   It is whispered from the mountaintops, for those with ears to hear.[140] Your death is a thing of the past, yet you yourselves have clearly not heard.

---

[137] Cf. Augustine, *City of God*, trans. Henry Bettenson (New York: Penguin, 1984), 440, 454.

[138] Cf. Matthew 23:27.

[139] Cf. Matthew 11:29.

Aceldama. Woe, woe.

Even so ye also outwardly appear righteous unto men, but within ye are full of hypocrisy and iniquity.[141] Ye appear righteous through the long lense of commercial media, your handmaiden. Ye appear righteous through the sound bite, the commercial announcement, the government spokesperson, the corporate PR firm, all glutted with your filthy lucre. You in your iniquity masquerade as an angel of light, as long ago.[142] Your righteousness is not as filthy rags: it simply is not.[143] As you bludgeon the righteous with the heel of your boot, you will evaporate as in a mist, transcending the ethereal. Prepare your embattlements. Ah, I have spoken too late.

Aceldama. Woe, woe.

Woe unto you, Cash Advancers and Title Loaners, hypocrites! Because ye build the tombs of the poor, the weak, the lame, the dumb, the sick, the mournful, the meek, the good, and garnish the wages and sepulchers of the righteous.[144] Woe, woe unto you for your shameless lust and covetousness. For you covet even the meager and clandestine happiness of the downtrodden and devise nefarious devices to rob them of even this, their final sustenance.

Aceldama. Woe, woe.

---

[140] Cf. Matthew 11:15.

[141] Cf. Matthew 23:28.

[142] Cf. II Corinthians 11:14.

[143] Cf. Isaiah 64:6.

[144] Cf. Matthew 23:29.

Woe unto you, Credit Card Companies and Usurious Lenders of the World, hypocrites! Because ye build the tombs of the desperate, the mentally ill, the addicted, the hopeless, the lonely, the broken hearted, the sorrowful, the good, and garnish the wages and sepulchers of the righteous.[145] Woe, woe unto you for your shameless gluttony wherein you seek to feast on all that is not yours. In your attempts to turn our planet into a moonscape, you will not be successful. *Aceldama. Woe, woe.*

Woe unto you, False Journalists and Bought Off Community Organizers, hypocrites! For your calling to heal and bring together and to speak truth to power, you have substituted an endless quest for self-aggrandizement and left those who needed your guidance to their own devices. Is it not clear that we needed you? That time was long past, and we need you no longer. We have found our own empowerment. The stench of your lies has reached the heavens. Your besotted mind has had its day of Tartuffery; now is the time to fall on your sword. *Aceldama. Woe, woe.*

Woe unto you, Union Breakers and Worker Desecrators, hypocrites! You are condemned for stealing from the worker her last shred of dignity--the right to say no to you--and you disguise this theft as a victory for the working people. Thus you rape, steal, and lie to the worker in your blind quest for profit upon profit as you crush first the souls and then the bodies of those you feign to empower. For you know that the difference between slavery and workers who cannot collectively bargain is a difference only in your favor.

---

[145] Cf. Matthew 23:29.

If the worker dies? So what? Collect your Dead Peasants Insurance and continue business as usual. We must notify you at this time that the game is now over and the planet is not big enough for the two of us. Don't like to be threatened? We say: so what? *Aceldama. Woe, woe.*

Woe unto you, False Prophets and Opportunistic Evangelists, hypocrites! You shove guilt and fear down the throats of the helpless, the destitute, the ignorant, the mournful, the friendless, and you do it in the name of God, all for your filthy mammon. How would it ever be that you could wash yourselves and atone for your sins? *Aceldama. Woe, woe.*

Woe unto you, Offshore Tax Evaders and Machinational Accountants, hypocrites! For as you hide your fenced lucre, so you lose your soul. Apparently, it is not something that you have missed. Your emptiness cries out for redress. The implosion is at hand. As you stuff your lucre into your undisclosed location, your carrion flesh reaches out to steal the crust from the mouth of a child. The child's eyes rest upon yours: you do not see. All that is not you, to you, is invisible. And yet...you do not exist. For she who has ears to hear, let her hear.[146] *Aceldama. Woe, woe.*

Woe unto you, Mortgage Executives and Adolf Eichmann paper pushers, hypocrites! For you grease the wheels of the machine of death and despair as you rationalize its necessity. Self-deception is now your only friend, and it is soon to forsake you. You will go mad with suffering, yet you will not know it. You will

---

[146] Cf. Mark 4:9.

continue to work intently on the amortization of your soul. When finished, the document will crumble as it touches your hands.

Aceldama. Woe, woe.

Woe unto you, Genetically Modified Proprietary Food Corporate Executives and Sellers of Water Rights, hypocrites! As you strip victuals from the innocent, so shall they be stripped from you. You will die of thirst and starvation within sight of them. They will be the last thing you see as you breathe your final breath. Alas, the victuals and water of life are of a proprietary nature. Someone else has legal rights to deprive you of them, for such rights exist, thanks to you, whereas a right to available water does not, nor does a right to available food. You, yes you, have created a world where no one has a right to life or even to the necessary preconditions for the possibility of a life, but the powerful have a right to deprive everyone else of the necessary preconditions for life. Thanks to you, the victualers of all of victualage the world over can be had for a price, and then you twist that which has been created into a form no less grotesque than you are yourselves. With the mammon you have stolen, you can buy them all, victualers the world over, and so silence the voices of the innocent. The voice of him that crieth in the wilderness[147]: the grass withereth, the flower fadeth, so ye shall fade into black.[148]

Aceldama. Woe, woe.

Woe unto you, Commanders of the Drones, with your latest extrajudicial instruments of terror, torture, and death. You who rule the skies with a mighty fist of

---

[147] Cf. Isaiah 40:3.

[148] Cf. Isaiah 40:8.

horror, you who excuse your evil in the name of freedom, democracy, human rights, peace. The terror of the drone will be with you all the days of your lives, and you shall dwell in the house of the drone forever.[149]

Aceldama. Woe, woe.

Woe unto you, Nuclear Power Executives and Natural Gas Corporate Moguls with your deadly radiation and your hydraulic fracturing, hypocrites! You travel over land and sea to rape the earth, and when you have done so, you say you are only providing a service, only meeting a demand.[150] What is the service that you provide, and what is the demand that you meet? Denial of the truth, death and destruction to all living things, wars and rumors of wars that enable you to continue raping *ad infinitum*?[151] Self-appointed Masters of the Material World, Big Daddies Suckin' at the Trough, it is you who deign yourselves worthy of such obscene pillage, and in deigning yourselves worthy you have unmistakably shown your unworthiness. Rape *ad infinitum*? It was just a misty dream of yours, in the days of wine and roses. Your path emerged for awhile. It will close within a dream.[152]

Aceldama. Woe, woe.

Woe unto you, Destroyers of Nature and Environmental Desecrators, hypocrites! For the price

---

[149] Cf. Psalm 23:6.

[150] Cf. Matthew 23:15.

[151] Matthew 24:6.

[152] Cf. Ernest Dowson, "They Are Not Long," *The Norton Anthology of English Literature*, Vol. 2, Sixth Edition, ed. M. H. Abrams (New York: W.W. Norton, 1993), 1681.

of a thousand year old sequoia, you will slay the forest. It does not cry out for mercy. Only the whisper of its voice is heard in the wind. For the price of the Amazon rainforest, you will destroy in days what took centuries, yea millennia, to come into being. You will not shed a tear, nor look back as your boot tramples the earth you have blasphemed. The blood of all our ancestors screams for the end to this unnature. You gloat only because you do not--cannot--hear the screaming.

Aceldama. Woe, woe.

Woe unto you, Soul Barterers of Compromised Religion and Metaphysical Profiteers, hypocrites! For twisting the voice of the spirit into your own voice, you will be recompensed. That which will be exacted you will neither be willing nor able to pay. Nonetheless, the verdict will stand, as did that of the banks who meted out injustice by stealing the widow's mite, her soul abode, along with her residence, her sole abode, while counting out their profits.[153]

Aceldama. Woe, woe.

Woe unto you, Human traffickers and Sellers of Human Rights, hypocrites, for as ye do unto others, so it shall be done unto you.[154] Ye have done it unto me, as ye have done it unto the least of my brethren: the leprous, those with HIV/AIDS, those with tuberculosis, those with cancer, the starving, the homeless, the jobless, those betrayed by family and friends, those that are shunned and discriminated against.[155] For

---

[153] Cf. Luke 21:1-4.

[154] Matthew 7:12, Luke 6:31.

[155] Matthew 25:40.

rusting treasure you will sell your brothers and sisters.[156] How is it that you can still be counted as one of us? Your visage will be absent as you peer into the mirror, an appropriate reflection of your absence of being. The time for change was...yesterday.

Aceldama. Woe, woe.

Woe unto you, Killers of Starving Babies and Killers of The Weak, The Blind, The Lame, The Dumb, The Mentally Handicapped, The Mentally Ill, hypocrites! For to you, the value of the least of your pleasures exceeds without question the worth of the least of these, my brethren.

Aceldama. Woe, woe.

Woe unto you, Creators of *Citizens United* and Supporters of The Unlimited Powers of The Corporate *Persona Ficta*, hypocrites! For your imaginary investment vehicles have made you glutted with opulence, and you have reaped where you have not sown.[157] For the legal institution of systemic violence against persons everywhere, you will be rewarded according to your just deserts. They shall look nothing like the deserts of those you have crushed, but for the first time, you will have earned them.

Aceldama. Woe, woe.

Woe unto you, Copious Polluters of Air and Water and Deniers of Global Warming, hypocrites! The blood of the children cries out to the third, fourth, tenth generation,[158] to see justice roll down like mighty

---

[156] Cf. Matthew 6:19.

[157] Matthew 25:24.

[158] Cf. Revelation 6:9-17.

waters upon you.[159]   The Grapes of Their Wrath will deluge your slothful gullet until you breathe no more.[160]

For your only real pleasure lies in destruction. Creation is as foreign to you as are life, truth, justice and mercy. You have not recognized mercy when it was shown unto you. It will be shown no longer.

Aceldama. Woe, woe.

Woe unto you, Perverters of The Arts and Sciences, and Attempted Perverters of All Truth and Knowledge, hypocrites! For merely a coin you have sold your soul to the untruth, and it is to the untruth that you will be beholden.   Would you enter into the same bargain again? Alas, the choice is merely hypothetical. The die is cast. Mendacity is your essence. Dialogue is no longer possible.   For it, you have attempted to substitute the communiqué.[161] Nevertheless, the wind blows where it will. You hear the sound of it, but you do not know where it comes from or where it is going.[162] So it is with those who refuse to bend their necks to your yoke of delusion, and they will never die.[163]

Aceldama. Woe, woe.

Woe unto you, Fighters For Injustice and Fighters For Unfreedom all around the world, hypocrites!   Your

---

[159] Amos 5:24.

[160] Cf. John Steinbeck, *The Grapes of Wrath* (New York: Penguin Classics, 2006).

[161] Cf. Albert Camus, *The Fall*, trans. Justin O'Brien (New York: Vintage, 1991), 45.

[162] John 3:8.

[163] Cf. Matthew 11:28-30.

conscience seared, you have lost your way. Who is there to lead you back to the light? The light for you is flickering. It is not long before the candle will be snuffed out.

All of you, all of you, all of you, all of you.

All of you would rather be judged by God than people such as yourselves.

You have judged for long enough. It is now the twilight of your idols.[164]

Ye serpents, ye generation of vipers, how can ye escape the damnation of the world?[165] No man can serve two masters: for either he will hate the one, and love the other; or else he will hold to the one and despise the other.[166] Even you, Masters of the Material World, Big Daddies Suckin' at the Trough, cannot serve humanity and mammon.[167] Oh, your travail at having to guide our lugubrious planet! The yoke must be heavy, the burden unlight![168] Ye have made your choice. Your golden calf is on high.[169] You raise your eyes to gaze upon that which you love so much! Humanity is no more than fuel for your hatred, a hatred that burns ceaselessly white. In your boundless hubris, you silently take credit for killing the divine, displacing the divine with yourselves--to you, a vast improvement.

---

[164] Friedrich Nietzsche, *Twilight of the Idols,* in *The Portable Nietzsche,* trans. Walter Kaufmann (New York: Penguin, 1977).

[165] Cf. Matthew 23:33.

[166] Cf. Luke 16:13.

[167] Cf. Matthew 6:24.

[168] Cf. Matthew 11:30.

[169] Cf. Exodus 32.

It is you who now surveil the planet, but not with loving eyes, save for your golden calf. Now you have gone further. It is humanity you have murdered, and even its possibility.

Zarathustra has spoken.[170]

How shall you ever comfort yourselves, the murderers of all murderers?[171] Do you even yet know that it is you above all who need comfort, but to no avail? How were you able to drink up the sea? It will not slake your thirst, as the brine eats you to nothing. What did you do, when you unchained this earth from its sun? What were you doing when you did anything you have done here on our god and man forsaken planet? Have you consciousness of any of your sordid deeds? Are you not constantly falling, plunging into the abyss of your own creation? Can you plunge any lower? Would it matter to you? Are you not wandering as through an infinite nothing? Are you not yourselves an infinite nothing mistaking itself for that greater than which none can be conceived?[172] Isn't the emptiness breathing upon you, its breath cold upon your crooked back? Or has emptiness become your new best friend? Isn't it colder, the heat of life a rapidly vanishing memory? Or is coldness your forever new homeostasis? Isn't the night coming for evermore--

---

[170] Cf. Friedrich Nietzsche, *Thus Spake Zarathustra: A Book for All and None,* trans. Walter Kaufmann (New York: Modern Library, 1995).

[171] This section utilizes Friedrich Nietzsche, *The Gay Science*, trans. Walter Kaufmann (New York: Vintage, 1974), Book Three, Section 125 ("The Madman"), 181–182. I am using a new translation by Kerstin Ellis as the basis for this section.

[172] Cf. Anselm's ontological argument in his *Proslogion,* as found in *From Plato to Derrida*, 5th edition, ed. Forrest E. Baird and Walter Kaufmann (Upper Saddle River, NJ: Pearson, 2008), 302-304.

and more night. Would you know the difference? Don't lanterns have to be lit in the morning? Only those with eyes left to see. Or is the morning itself gone forever? Is there no sound?

Do we not hear the noise of the gravediggers, straining to bury humanity? Only those with ears left to hear. Do we smell nothing as yet of the holy decay, the decomposition of our own being? Death smells like life to you: hence the inexorable attraction. Humanity is dead, and you have killed humanity.

There will be no comfort for you, the murderers of all murderers. The holiest and mightiest the world possessed, bled to death through the use of your knives. There is no one to wipe the blood from you or from your knives; it has become inexpungible. What kind of water could clear you? There is no water for you to clean yourselves. The water shall henceforth remain forever out of reach. Furthermore, the stains are indelible. Your festivals and sacred games are over; you shall no longer live on the blood of the sacrificial lamb of humanity. There is no propitiation for your sin, there is no forgiveness for your evil, there is no redemption for your misdeeds, there is no understanding for your actions. There is only horror without end. Is only horror without end. Only horror without end. Horror without end. Without end. End. *Aceldama. Woe, woe. Apollyon.*[173]

Wherefore, behold, I send unto you prophets of truth, and wise men, and wise women, and chroniclers and voracious narrators of veracity: and some of them you shall kill outright, and others you will send to Guantanamo or Abu Ghraib or to one of the other

---

[173] Revelation 9:11.

dozens of undisclosed black sites all around the globe in countries that don't mind torturing and disappearing, if the price is right.[174] Or Quantico.

Habeas Corpus isn't for losers, you say. Imprison, torture, kill in the name of freedom, for the gods of wealth and power, nostrils breathing hot for the kill. You have lost your way, my friend. And you have stopped your ears against the prophets of truth for so long that you no longer know that all you hear is the sound of your own voice. You are lost in a solipsistic universe of endless soliloquy, a boundless monologue, a forced march to oblivion. A pastoral on the prison cell is your call of freedom.[175] Your mind is terminally twisted.[176] You've got the insatiable lust that requires blood sacrifice. Ye know not what you do. For your blood sport disguised as liberation, you will be smitten.

Aceldama. Woe, woe.

That upon you may come all the righteous blood shed upon the earth; upon the earth all the righteous blood shed upon you will come.[177] It is a sea of blood, vaster than the widest ocean, beyond comprehension, a sea of blood shed by you, Masters of the Material World, Big Daddies Suckin' at the Trough. You sacrifice whatever does not serve your mighty plan. Your delusional plan is a tale told by idiots, full of sound and fury, signifying nothing.[178]

---

[174] Cf. Matthew 23:34.

[175] Cf. Albert Camus, *The Fall*, trans. Justin O'Brien (New York: Vintage, 1991), 123-124.

[176] Cf. The Eagles: "Hotel California" (1976).

[177] Cf. Matthew 23:35.

For absence is your ontology, and you create in your own image, a creation that is an absence of creation, a footprint that is an endless black hole, a gaping, cavernous antithesis of being. Everyone that is of the truth heareth my voice.[179] You are already ghosts; pass on to the land of Sheol,[180] to the land of Gehenna,[181] to Abaddon.[182] Death merchants: leave the earth to the living.

Aceldama. Woe, woe.

Verily I say unto you, all these things shall come upon this generation, Generation Omega, the last generation prior to the liberation of the planet, a generation of enlightened ones who have groaned under the yoke of evil for time enough. For the true spirit of liberty ariseth among the people, the many crushed and beaten down by the few. Behold, enslavers and merchants of death: your house is left unto you desolate. You are all parasites. Your host will now destroy you. You will be laid waste. It is written on the hearts of the children of men.

Do not think that we have come to reason with you. Feigned ratiocination is one of your favorite weapons. The time for reasoning together is over. It was always merely a game for you. So once again we say unto

---

[178] Shakespeare, *Macbeth,* Act V, Scene V.

[179] Cf. John 18:37.

[180] Hebrew land of the dead, underworld.

[181] Hell, or place of extreme torment and suffering, originally the valley of Hinnom where children were sacrificed to Baal or Moloch. See II Kings 23:10, Jeremiah 19:5-6.

[182] Destruction, or hell.

you: do not think that we have come to reason with you.

We have come to philosophize, but only with a hammer.[183] With a hammer we will smash every idol you have fashioned to imprison us. With a hammer we will smash every idol you have fashioned to cause us to live in fear. With a hammer we will smash every idol you have fashioned to deceive us into giving to you our blood, sweat, and tears. With a hammer we will smash every idol you have fashioned to corrupt our powers of reason and perception. With a hammer we will smash every idol you have fashioned to destroy our souls. And when we have finished smashing every idol you have fashioned, we will then turn our hammer upon you and justice will roll down like mighty waters, righteousness like an everlasting stream.[184]

---

[183] Cf. Friedrich Nietzsche, *Twilight of the Idols,* in *The Portable Nietzsche,* trans. Walter Kaufmann (New York: Penguin, 1977).

[184] Cf. Amos 5:24.

CHAPTER FIFTEEN

TERRORISM AS A TOOL OF THE INTERNATIONAL POWER ELITE

It was just another day of the same old same old. School, long run with the guys, and the walk back home in the fading twilight. His mom wasn't home yet and his dad was in the recliner in front of the TV watching some old Western. Tommie finished off what was left of somebody's refrigerated macaroni and cheese and found himself at loose ends. He said "Hi" to his dad and went upstairs to his bedroom.

Tommie knew he had a reading assignment for tomorrow's philosophy class. He also knew that if he didn't read the assignment, the odds were that Winter would call on him, and things would go downhill from there. Winter's class was nerve wracking enough as it was--in a mostly good way--but still, he didn't want to push his luck. The Blue Dog Clint Eastwood Bette Davis eyes transfixed upon him? No thanks. Too harrowing to contemplate. He'd rather run twenty kilometers naked through quicksand. Besides, he actually liked the readings, even if he didn't always know if he had a clue about what the hell was going on in the text. Usually he did, but he wasn't sure enough of himself to know that he did.

The readings were short by most standards--ten to fifteen pages--but Tommie realized early on that ten or fifteen pages of dense philosophical reading could easily take him as long as fifty or even one hundred pages of fiction, and his comprehension on the shorter reading could be, shall we say, less than ideal.

Being the cross-country runner that he was, this provided a challenge. It was a challenge that he, of course, could not pass up. Masochism is a hard habit to break. Especially for the masochist. It was early, and for once he wasn't tired. An opportune time for the philosophical reading, in more than one way. If it was like most philosophical readings, it was a better soporific than a handful of sleeping pills. He needed something to take his mind off of everything that was going on. His dad, his mom, Monica's mother, cross-country season--he was starting to feel the weight of the suffering around him. He was even thinking about Harlan's dad and the debt consolidation scam. He propped three pillows against the wall and jumped on his bed. He slid the computer off of his nightstand and logged on to the course. It was only 8:14. Winter often posted supplementary reading assignments on the course site. Tommie located the reading for the day. He began reading.

TERRORISM AS A TOOL OF THE INTERNATIONAL POWER ELITE, WITH SPECIAL ATTENTION TO THE USE OF INVISIBLE VIOLENCE

RUTHERFORD URIAS AUGUSTUS WINTER, Ph.D.[185]

---

[185] A fictitious character, one of the protagonists in my trilogy *The Terror of the Simulacra* (Ozark Mountain Writers Guild), forthcoming.

Terrorism is violence, but it does not require overt physical violence or terror as they are traditionally understood. It is a tool, a technique utilized by identified and unidentified individuals and collectives to manipulate and control a targeted group of people. Terror, as such, is the mechanism by which terrorists exert control. Terrorism is a teleological procedure designed to control a given subgroup. Its aims transcend terror, thus terror is not the goal of terrorism. Its aims transcend physical violence, thus physical violence is not the goal of terrorism. It may even be stated that physical violence against the targeted group may be neither a necessary nor a sufficient condition to effect the aims of the terrorist organization in question, and may, in fact, be contraindicated. As such, neither conscious terror nor physical violence are required to effect the teleology of terror.

The principles of parsimony and coversion necessitate a minimum of physical violence, stressing instead the advantages of subliminal psychological violence against the intended victims. This is often most successfully accomplished through the induction of a radical sense of insecurity within the targeted population. To this end, all historically necessary means of self-preservation practiced by the targeted group must be destabilized, including but not limited to food, housing, energy, medical care, education, work, culture, leisure, and political enfranchisement and liberties.

Let us speak briefly of the United States of America with regard to these issues. Within the sphere of work, there is neither job security, collective bargaining or any other significant enforceable rights, nor any type of meaningful compensation should one find oneself jobless. Outsourcing, subcontracting, downsizing, rightsizing, and the use of undocumented workers serve to keep the wages of those "lucky" enough to remain employed at a subsistence level and to keep workers on edge, lest they be the next to go. Worker solidarity is replaced with acrimony, animosity and, above all, suspicion.

As wages are driven down through induced insecurity, workers are increasingly forced to utilize institutions such as credit card conglomerates, payday lenders and title loan companies to maintain equilibrium. These lenders, without exception, charge usurious rates, rates effectively set by the international power elite. Meanwhile, the CEOs, CFOs, Members of the Board of Directors and other elites at these same firms are rewarded with millions, even as they lay workers off, drive wages down, and run companies into the ground.

Within the sphere of housing, the lender utilizes the mortgage acceleration clause to radically destabilize the market, allowing for the legal seizure of collateral without significant legal recourse for the persons who actually live in the home. This clause, rarely noted at any time during the transaction, allows the lender to call in the entire loan, often if the borrower is only a few days behind on the payment. The reason the borrower is behind (job loss, reduction in work hours, cancer, heart attack, stroke, death in family, suicide, military deployment, car accident, flood, fire, war, nuclear reactor meltdown, hurricane, tsunami, earthquake, terrorist attack) is irrelevant; the loan can be called in and another nameless someone will become homeless.

This produces yet another sense of radical insecurity. At one stroke, the lender regains the collateral, keeps all monies paid, resells the property, and keeps rental prices high (the nameless someone must reside somewhere—one would think—but in such a radically destabilized market, even this is not guaranteed). A stroke of terroristic genius—if you're the one with the money. But it doesn't stop there. These same power elites can then transfer these monies to offshore accounts in the Caribbean or the Mediterranean or into secret

Swiss bank accounts, accounts protected by these same elites from the Internal Revenue Service. Only those who do not have the connections to allow for such foreign accounts must actually pay federal income taxes. If you are working for these elites as a fund manager on these accounts and have specific inside information on those breaking the law and you blow the whistle, you will be arrested and tried. Or simply arrested and not tried, but plea-bargained into silence and obscurity. The accounts will remain secret. The elites are self-exempting.

Since they also control legislation, including tax law, the situation is relatively stable for the power elite, allowing them to defund any federal or state program deemed by them to run counter to their teleology of induced radical insecurity in the targeted population (including defunding any program deemed too "educational"). Within the sphere of education, we see the power elite rewriting "education" policy to coincide with their corporate agenda, an agenda that institutionalizes subliminal terror as natural law, producing, if possible, a fully predictable herd animal. Such rewriting includes the colleges and universities that would traditionally have been in a position to dismantle the fictitious narrative of the power elite as they seek complete dominion over what passes for truth and knowledge. Finally, the Supreme Court decision in *Citizens United* completes the disenfranchisement and ensures the thoroughgoing muting of the voice of the subjected group. Legal and human rights no longer exist for the terrorized group, the group that comprises a minimum of 99% of the societal population. Recognition and internalization of this reality augments and solidifies the terror within the targeted group.

Thus we see that (transitory and ephemeral) governments are merely an epiphenomenon of the goals and interests of the international power elite. These goals and interests are advanced through the institution of a fully monetized economy. To effect this end, local nonmonetized traditional barter and trade economies must be destabilized and subverted via the introduction of monetization through organizations such as the International Monetary Fund and the World Bank, institutions which radically destabilize traditional homeostatic economies, undermine participatory government, and destroy the rule of law.

Add to this the inscrutable privately held Federal Reserve and the invisible violence perpetrated against the 99% is complete. The Federal Reserve is not accountable to any arm of government and operates with nearly complete opacity. It can print money and buy worthless fictions that are referred to as complex investment vehicles—all invented by the power elite—paying billions of dollars for these empty vessels. Thus the Federal Reserve transfers billions directly to the power elite in exchange for whatever accoutrements of power and privilege deemed by these same elites as timely and appropriate. The unconscionable raping of the working people goes unnoticed—for their needs, desires, rights, hopes, dreams and victuals are invisible to the power elite— except to the degree that they interfere with the teleology of this elite.

Meanwhile, those that actually work for a living are increasingly required to utilize the commercial lending system in order to keep up with basic payments to secure lodging, transportation, clothing, food and health care. This group is additionally violated by being held hostage to the credit score, another invention of the power elite, something now utilized by them not only for lending to the targeted group, but for insurance and even employment as well. The credit score may be accurately described as an individual compliance rating, or a docility factor.

At the same time, it must appear to the targeted group that those ostensibly in charge are doing everything they can to guarantee stabilization and equity in all of the aforementioned areas. Propaganda is the surest means to effect this end. Propaganda can take many forms: economic forecasts, weather forecasts, education, religion, worker's rights (this is particularly notable in "right to work" states), science, politics, culture. The common denominator: to be effective, propaganda cannot be seen as such, but rather, it must pass for the truth. The lie as truth is the technical commodification of terror, the requisite product by which an international post-industrial power elite subvert any purported democratic process. This would include the purported democratic process as currently installed in the United States of America, a prima facie constitutional republic. The military defense of this pseudo-inclusive nation state is relegated to the terrorized targeted group (who "volunteer" for service, many of whom have few or no other viable options), while the power elite dictate the terms.

Multinational corporate conglomerates who sell lies as truth produce the necessary and sufficient conditions to ensure the ongoing subversion of human rights and the democratic process, provided that the potential truths revealed through societal educational systems have been sufficiently propagandized. Put differently, the lie will be portrayed as "truth" through these pseudo-educational programs. Thus, the question of truth does not arise. This dually constituted program of propaganda, with its arms of news and education, thereby effectively seals the targeted environment from the contamination of truth. Truth would mitigate and attenuate the intended program of control through terror and must therefore be minimized, maligned, eliminated.

Control of information and therefore thought, to the degree that such is possible, requires control of all substantive media sources, including the Internet. The power elite in both Egypt and Libya recognized this long before the uprisings of 2011, but overt suspension of access was required as the movement of insurgency gained momentum. So it is with the power elite on every continent, regardless of the officially stated form of government (a position which in itself represents a subset of the campaign of misinformation).[186] Sufficient control of information—lie as truth—is required in order to induce and control the prescriptive amount of terror, based upon the aims of the power elite. Even the thought or memory of terror may be sufficient to terrorize a given population, in which case the power elite have little to do but reinforce the simmering hysteria.

Historically, the aims of the power elite in every case run counter to the demonstrable interests of the non-elites.[187] If they did not, the entire project of terror and control would be superfluous. The power elite rule through an unholy alliance of government and business (a subset being the business of religion), an alliance that produces the bureaucratic medical-military-industrial-complex.

---

[186] That is, the stated form or type of government is in itself a form of propaganda, given that the power elite have always had a universal disdain for the sharing of power, relegating it only to themselves. The popular notion of bringing others into the umbrella of shared governance (as is purportedly the case in a democracy or a republic) is itself a fiction designed and promulgated by the power elite.

[187] This is the case only in regard to the power elite qua power elite. In cases where the elites seek the collective good, their interests are no longer antithetical to those of the non-elites. An inductive analysis of history clearly shows that instances of this type are so rare as to be anomalous, so the present analysis will proceed without regard to them. In such cases, adjustments will have to be made, but let the reader be cautioned that situations in which the power elite seek the collective good are highly unstable and may fall back into *normal hegemonic socio-economic conditions* at any time—conditions in which the elites exploit all others as much through their power as through the idealistic delusions of the non-elites. These delusions, of course, are generated and fostered by the power elite. They include belief in the possibility of socio-economic equality and equality of opportunity.

The government and military are subsets of the international business interests of the elite, an elite which utilizes the concepts of patriotism, human rights, freedom and democracy as tools to advance its interests without regard for the things themselves. Or rather, with flagrant disregard for the things themselves to the degree that patriotism, human rights, freedom and democracy interfere with the interests of said group.

Such a medical-military-industrial complex requires constant war or the simulacra of war as a tool of terror. Additionally, the elites that generate this multifarious complex need to dismantle any constitutionally protected rights in the name of said war. Terror and control would be incompletely realized without the double effect of endless war and the attendant stripping of all guarantees of human rights in the name of said war. Real war, then, is not a necessity, just as reality, as such, is not a necessity.

To go further: reality itself is a luxury the terrorists cannot afford. Or, to be more precise, reality is useful only to the extent that it can be utilized to go beyond itself to produce a manageable unreality that can be imposed upon the targeted group.   Reality, per se, is an impediment to the propagandization of reality and therefore must be concealed while at the same time being conceptually amplified. The concept of reality has endless functionality in the hands of the power elite. At the same time, the incipient encroachment of reality must be eliminated by any means necessary and in accordance with the principles of parsimony and coversion.

A current example of such an aversion to truth is the reaction of the government of the United States of America to Julian Assange and the Wikileaks website. Reality is in contradistinction to the aim of the terrorists, as their ultimate telos is the manufacture and control of reality (lie as truth) as such. To this end, all discourse must be regulated. No unsanctioned discourse is allowed.

The objectives of said terrorists (the controllers of the medical-military-industrial complex) are at odds with principles of freedom, democracy, and human rights. This group currently seeks extradition of Assange, a move designed to benefit their own terrorist agenda, a Machiavellian agenda at odds with the principles of freedom, democracy, and human rights.[188] The narration requires only that reality exist as a background concept. This formula is replicated *ad infinitum*. The faces change; the game remains the same. No unsanctioned discourse is allowed.

The simulacrum of war is generally a sufficient condition for the elites to control the targeted group through terror. The power elite can, of course, benefit from real war in two ways: economic gain and propaganda-induced loyalty/patriotism. Terror as a tool to subvert the interests of the targeted population in favor of the interests of the international power elite is the most closely guarded secret of this class. The first order of business for the power elite is to produce in the terrorized the belief that the power elite does not exist. Having successfully induced disbelief in said class, the question of terror as a tool of a nonexistent class does not arise. If those controlled remain noncognizant of their own induced (rather than existential) terror, no explanation is required. If the controlled become aware of their terror and determine that it is induced, some explanation is required.

Thus the need for a war on terror. This war must exist as long as terror recognized as such exists. Terror must be endless, as a built-in requirement generated by the existence of the power elite. Terror recognized as such will remain only a contingent condition to be exploited as deemed necessary by the power elite.

Once terror is recognized as such, the question of the origin of

---

[188] See Niccolò Machiavelli, *The Prince,* trans. N.H. Thomson.

(Mineola, NY: Dover Publications, 1992).

terror will never arise, since it is already deemed to be addressed in the object of the war on terror. Such an object, of course, is anything but the origin of the terror the controlled group seeks to extinguish (at the behest of the elite) through said war on terror.

To repeat, the goal is control and manipulation through the technique of terrorism. This is best achieved by means other than direct physical assault, yet all terrorism is a form of violence. It strips those targeted of the possibility of a life of self-determination. It denies fundamental human rights and is one of the highest forms of disrespect against human life. Finite terror can be produced through physical and systemic violence. Infinite terror can be induced through propaganda and the attendant destruction of educational systems within the targeted group. Psychic terrorism is homicide by other means. It generates ubiquitous terror, a situation in which even the notion of self-protection is defunct, since self-protection is no longer possible. The victims of such ubiquitous induced terror, having no visible means of recourse, end by embracing the very group that induces said terror.

Thus the targeted group embraces and precipitates its own terror, its own demise, in the name of self-preservation. It drinks the poison, looking upon it as the antidote to that very poison. Within such a fully propagandized pseudoreality, there is no clear Archimedean point from which to leverage oneself and one's peers beyond the propaganda. Consciousness of the process of terror as a tool of the power elite is a necessary but insufficient condition to create fertile ground for democracy, human rights, and real freedom for all peoples. The front of such a real war on terror is fought on the fringes of human consciousness. The question here becomes notably broader: how does one bring to awareness that of which one is not aware, especially given that from one's perspective of non-awareness, one will generally infer that there is nothing about which one must become aware? Still, if one recognizes the possibility of such non-awareness, this does not for that reason induce awareness. But it is a movement toward the light.

These concerns raise larger questions concerning the nature of human consciousness, including but not limited to the question of self-deception. Within the realm of self-deception, the phenomenon of the Stockholm syndrome has particular relevance to our present discussion. These issues are beyond the scope of our present narration, and must therefore await a later elucidation. An exposition and analysis of self-deception and its subset, the Stockholm syndrome, are necessary to the full understanding of terror as a tool of the international power elite. At this juncture, we shall turn to a specific example of terror as a tool of the international power elite, with particular reference to induced terror through the use of invisible systemic violence.

Many specific concrete examples could be offered to demonstrate that the power elite utilize terror as a tool to control and manipulate the non-elite. From "too big to fail" corporate monoliths to the absence of habeas corpus, to dragnet data mining without the need for warrant or justification, to arbitrary curbs on free speech and free assembly, to Supreme Court verdicts installing American presidents, multiple and pervasive constructed scenarios serve to undermine the very possibility of peace and to induce terror.

Let us take the absence of universal health care as one example among others, for this reality is a quintessential example of control through terror utilizing the principles of parsimony and coversion, a situation that clearly serves the international interests of the power elite. To begin, we must make a clear distinction between health insurance and health care, since the former is certainly no guarantee of the latter.

Health insurance, per se, is simply not a guarantee of health care, but may in fact in some instances serve as a deterrent to health care. This discussion will focus instead on health care.

Without a minimal level of guaranteed access to health care, a population lives with radical insecurity, a sense of insecurity well described by Thomas Hobbes in his LEVIATHAN (1652) as the state of nature, a state prior to the time in which a human being lives in a civil society, a society which would provide certain guarantees against the expected exigencies of solitary living.[189] One primary focus of civil and social society should be to alleviate the existential terror of everyday living through the sharing of resources, knowledge, power, and defenses.   But a society where anyone is potentially one serious illness away from destitution, poverty, homelessness, starvation and death is certainly not a civil society by any account.

Put differently: a society that would allow anyone to lose anything and everything necessary to sustain human life when such a situation is eminently preventable does not meet the necessary preconditions for civil society. No one would agree to such a situation in John Rawls' hypothetical original position, wherein we choose the basic framework of justice as fairness without knowing where we will be in the socio-economic hierarchy, since this situation is neither fair nor just by any account other than that of the specious narration of the power elite.[190]   A society where anyone is potentially one serious illness away from destitution, poverty, homelessness, starvation and death is certainly not a civil society by any account, and yet such is the present situation in the United States of America.

---

[189] Thomas Hobbes, *Leviathan or the Matter, Form, and Power of a Commonwealth, Ecclesiastical or Civil.* See especially Part I, Chapters 12-15 and Part II, Chapters 17, 18, and 21.

[190] John Rawls, *A Theory of Justice* (Boston: Harvard University Press, 1971).

Such an uncivil situation clearly violates multiple articles of the *Universal Declaration of Human Rights*, adopted by the United Nations General Assembly on December 10, 1948. At that time, the Assembly called upon all member nations to publish and disseminate the thirty articles found in the *Declaration*, and "to cause it to be disseminated, displayed, read, and expounded principally in schools and other educational institutions, without distinction based on the political status of countries or territories." I will note only portions of two articles of the *Universal Declaration of Human Rights*, the content of which the United States is in clear violation, given the aforementioned regarding health care:

Article 3: "Everyone has the right to life, liberty and security of person."

Article 25 (1): "Everyone has a right to a standard of living adequate for the health and well-being of himself and of his family, including food, clothing, housing and medical care and necessary social services, and the right to security in the event of unemployment, sickness, disability, widowhood, old age or other lack of livelihood in circumstances beyond his control."

It is eminently clear that Americans have no such rights. For this reason as well as those drawn from Hobbes and Rawls, we see that America is in fact not a civil society at all. Such a situation is one of induced terror. It is a situation of systemic invisible violence inducing terror, based upon the principles of parsimony and coversion.

With few exceptions, economics rather than need is the determining factor when it comes to the availability of health care in the United States. Thousands die, sustain preventable permanent injuries, are made homeless or lose all of their savings and/or incur monstrous debt every year due to medical reasons in these United States of America, a country that gave hundreds of billions of dollars in bailouts to the very Wall Street robber baron financiers that precipitated the crisis that "required" the bailouts. The overt agenda of the power elite was operative here (placing them in a potentially vulnerable position), yet the dual propaganda campaign of commercial media and educational institutions was so successful in this instance that many of those terrorized praised the bailouts—immediately after the largest transfer of wealth in world history—as the right thing to do.

Meanwhile, tens of millions who work every day, year in and year out, could lose everything in an instant if they were in an automobile accident and required sustained medical attention (even if they were not at fault). This is an artificially created state of nature, a state of war of every man against every man, a state of terror. Pervasive terror is thus induced from the ubiquitous and seemingly irremediable artificially created situation of constitutive instability, a situation that cannot be rectified even in theory as long as the unstated fundamental tenets that precipitated the situation are not addressed.   The putative intractability of the current egregiously unjust situation is part of the mythology of the power elites.

To return to Thomas Hobbes in LEVIATHAN: "To this war of every man against every man this also is consequent, that nothing can be unjust. The notions of right and wrong, justice and injustice, have there no place. Where there is no common power, there is no law; where no law, no injustice."[191] Hobbes goes on to assert that the terror of such a state is far greater than the terror of a unitary dictatorship, and yet we are in such a state. The existing artificially created state of nature is nothing less than a state of induced terror.

Nothing can be unjust: neither death, nor famine, nor poverty, nor homelessness, since the onus to provide these essentials rests squarely upon the person who sustained serious injury in the aforementioned automobile accident, through no fault of her own. No one owes her a thing, not even

_____

[191] Thomas Hobbes, *Leviathan*, Chapter 13.

to be left to die peacefully—from preventable injuries—on a public sidewalk, since "living" in said location could very well violate local ordinances. Nothing can be unjust: the denial of a medical procedure necessary for continued existence on planet Earth—if the patient in question has not made acceptable financial arrangements. Meanwhile, multimillion dollar bonuses to executives at the bailed out criminal syndicates on Wall Street and around the world must be paid due to "contractual obligation". Nothing can be unjust. Nothing can be unjust in the state of nature, since conditions do not yet obtain for justice to exist.

These conditions exist by design, as they provide the constitutive instability necessary to induce terror unrecognized as such. The targeted group cowers under the weight of the onslaught of the contradictory nature of its reality, a reality where freedom is trumpeted from every rooftop by the relentless corporate media and the corporate institutions of indoctrination that pass for schools and colleges and universities, while feeling somehow that it cannot find terra firma, that nothing is sacred because nothing is protected, that nothing is sacred because everything is negotiable, that nothing is sacred because everything is for sale. When nothing is sacred, the people, as such, perish.

The notion of a common destiny, the notion of brotherhood, the notion of sisterhood, the notion of statehood, the notion of statecraft, the notion of community, they are gone, gone in a sea of calculated verbiage. Living together has been replaced with competition unto death. In the final analysis, when nothing is sacred, the individual ceases to exist. The very possibility of personhood is eradicated. The use of systemic invisible violence as a tool of terror by the power elite makes it all possible. Hail to the new Masters of the Universe. The King is dead. Long live the King.

N.B. To all students: If you do not understand a vocabulary word, look it up and learn it.

Tommie closed his computer and slipped it under the bed, then got up to take a leak. It was only 9:37 but he was exhausted. He had actually managed to finish the reading. He stumbled back to bed and turned out the nightstand lamp. Soon the waves of fitful sleep were crashing over the embers of his consciousness.

ACKNOWLEDGMENTS

Many claim that writing is by nature a solitary pursuit. In my experience, this has been anything but the case. The people who have influenced, supported, and encouraged me--and have often led the way--are certainly the most important reasons why this book exists (I know, some may consider this a bad thing). To all of my former colleagues at Rhodes College in Memphis, Tennessee, I thank you for all that you have done for me over many years--and for so many things that I have forgotten: Patrick Shade, Robert Llewellyn, Joe Favazza, Brendan O'Sullivan, Maria Talero, Brian Warren, Kathleen Doyle, Katheryn Wright, David Sick, Mike Witek, Mark Smith, Tom Bremer, John Kaltner, David Jilg, Mike LaRosa, Jim Vest, Don Tucker, Bernadette McNary-Zak, Mark Muesse, David Mason, Pete and Carol Ekstrom, Kathy Foreman, Rosanna Capellato, Mimi Atkinson, Ming Dong Gu, Eric Gottlieb, Horst Dinkelacker, María Ballinger, Rocio Rodriquez del Rio, Kathleen Laakso, Eric Henager, Mike Nelson, Milton Moreland, Steve Ceccoli, Frank Mora, Katherine Panagakos, Doug Hatfield, Larry Lacy, Judith Haas, Joe Jansen, Marilyn Hury, Susan Kus, Valeria Nollan, Michelle Mattson, Shira Malkin, Patrick Gray, Dan Cullen, Gail Murray, Alexandra "Sasha" Kostina, Nora Jabbour, John Ross, Bette Ackerman, Chris Wetzel, and Gail Streete.

I would also like to thank Dr. Richard J. Westley, Loyola University Chicago, and Dr. John Ellsworth Winter, Millersville University, both mentors and friends.

At the University of Memphis, I would like to thank Ken and Mona Kreitner as well as Doug Lemmon.

Thank you as well to Tim O'Donnell, Karen Granda, and Lisa Brock of the School of the Art Institute of Chicago, Brian Bilderback of Columbia College - Missouri, and Steve Asma of Columbia College - Chicago.

Additionally, I would like to thank poet Daniel Ladinsky for his inspiration, friendship and encouragement. He knew just what to say and when to say it.

I would also like to thank philosopher Chris Broniak for his invaluable reading and editorial skills. Thank you to Nancy Owen Barton for her helpful suggestions and encouragement.

To Baylor University, Loyola University Chicago, Columbia College Chicago, The School of the Art Institute of Chicago, The American Conservatory of Music, The University of Memphis, Christian Brothers University, Rhodes College, Drury University, and Columbia College Missouri--thank you.

To all my friends in Missouri--Chris Jocius, George McPherson, Lynne Weixel, Gary Sewell, Dulce and Ken Alford, Joan Aronstam--thank you for your critical minded probity. Thank you as well to Carolyn Ellis and Sarah, James and Sam Swindell.

Thank you to Roberto Irwin for tech support and Nina Irwin for aesthetic input.

Thank you to Myra Miller, Tuesday Florence and Candy Pitman at Drury University, Rolla Campus. They have been known to surmount the insurmountable.

To all my students over these last twenty-seven years, thank you for making this planet a better place. It has been a pleasure to know you.

Above all, to my readers: may you continue to reflect and work to take the hard and better road, a road that may allow our species to live but a longer moment on this hurtling sphere.

Finally, for hours of solicited (and unsolicited) input, for years of patience and support, and for all the intangible things that I could never express on the page, I thank my wife, Dr. Amanda Lee Irwin.

For those that I have failed to mention, I do apologize. For this oversight, as well as for those that are bound to exist in this work, I take full responsibility.

SELECT BIBLIOGRAPHY AND RECOMMENDED RESOURCES

Anonymous. *The Epic of Gilgamesh*. Trans. Andrew George. New York: Penguin, 1999.

Anonymous. *The Epic of Gilgamesh*. Trans. N. K. Sandars. New York: Penguin, 1972.

Aquinas, Thomas. *Introduction to St. Thomas Aquinas: The Summa Theologica and the Summa Contra Gentiles*. Ed. Anton C. Pegis. New York: Modern Library, 1948.

Aristotle. *Nicomachean Ethics*. 2nd Edition. Trans. Terence Irwin. Indianapolis: Hackett, 2009.

Augustine. *City of God*. Trans. Henry Bettenson. New York: Penguin, 1984.

Bamford, James. *The Shadow Factory: The NSA From 9/11 to the Eavesdropping on America*. New York: Anchor, 2009.

Benjamin, Medea. *Drone Warfare: Killing By Remote Control*. Brooklyn, NY: Verso, 2013.

Blair, James, Derek Mitchell and Karina Blair. *The Psychopath: Emotion and the Brain*. Malden, MA: Blackwell Publishing, 2005.

Albert Camus. *The Fall*. Trans. Justin O'Brien. New York: Vintage, 1991.

----------. *The Rebel: An Essay on Man in Revolt*. Trans. Anthony Bower. New York: Vintage, 1956.

Chomsky, Noam. *Hopes and Prospects*. Chicago: Haymarket Books, 2010.

Coogan, Michael D., Ed. Marc Z. Brettler, Carol Newsom and Pheme Perkins, Ass. Eds. *The New Oxford Annotated Bible*, Third Edition. New Revised Standard Version. New York: Oxford University Press, 2007.

Crane, Stephen. *The Red Badge of Courage*. *The Complete Novels of Stephen Crane*. Ed. Thomas A. Gullason. Garden City, NY: Doubleday and Company, 1967.

Dostoyevsky, Fyodor. *Notes From the Underground*. Trans. Constance Garnett. Mineola, NY: Dover Publications, 1992.

Ehle, John. *Trail of Tears: The Rise and Fall of the Cherokee Nation*. New York: Anchor Books, 1989.

Friedrich, Otto. *The Kingdom of Auschwitz*. New York: HarperPerennial, 1982.

The Gideons International. *The New Testament With Psalms and Proverbs.* Authorized King James Version. Nashville: National Publishing Company, 1968.

Greenwald, Glenn. *With Liberty and Justice for Some: How the Law is Used to Destroy Equality and Protect the Powerful.* London: Picador, 2012.

Gregg, Richard B. *The Value of Voluntary Simplicity.* Wallingford, PA: Pendle Hill Publications, 1936.

Hare, Robert D. *Without Conscience: The Disturbing World of the Psychopaths Among Us.* New York: The Guilford Press, 1999.

Hastings, Michael. *The Operators: The Wild and Terrifying Inside Story of America's War in Afghanistan.* New York: Blue Rider Press, 2012.

Hedges, Chris. *Death of the Liberal Class.* New York: Nation Books, 2010.

Hume, David. *An Enquiry Concerning Human Understanding.* Mineola, NY: Dover Publications, 2004.

----------. *Treatise of Human Nature.* Ed. T.H. Green and T. H. Grose. London: Longmans, Green, and Co., 1886.

Huxley, Aldous. *Brave New World.* New York: Harper and Brothers, 1932.

Johnston, David Kay. *Perfectly Legal: The Covert Campaign to Rig Our Tax System to Benefit the Super Rich – and Cheat Everyone Else*. New York: Portfolio Trade, 2003, updated 2005.

Kafka, Franz. *The Trial*. Trans. David Wyllie. Mineola, NY: Dover Publications, 2003.

Kant, Immanuel. *Groundwork of the Metaphysics of Morals*. Trans. H.J. Paton. New York: Harper Perennial, 2009.

Kierkegaard, Søren [Johannes Climacus]. *The Concluding Unscientific Postscript to the Philosophical Fragments*. Trans. David F. Swenson and Walter Lowrie. Princeton, NJ: Princeton University Press, 1968.

Kuttner, Robert. *Everything For Sale: The Virtues and Limits of Markets*. New York: Alfred A. Knopf, 1998.

Lem, Stanislaw. *The Futurological Congress*. Trans. Michael Kandel. New York: Avon, 1974.

Lunn, Pam. *Costing Not Less Than Everything: Sustainability and Spirituality in Challenging Times*. The 2011 Swarthmore Lecture. London: Quaker Books, 2011.

Machiavelli, Niccolò. *The Prince*. Trans. N.H. Thomson. Mineola, NY: Dover Publications, 1992.

MacPherson, Myra. *"All Governments Lie": The Life and Times of Rebel Journalist I. F. Stone*. New York: Scribner, 2008.

Mill, John Stuart. *On Liberty*. Ed. Elizabeth Rapaport. Indianapolis: Hackett: 1978.

----------. *Utilitarianism*. 2nd Edition. Ed. George Sher. Indianapolis: Hackett, 2001.

Miller, Alice. *Thou Shalt Not Be Aware: Society's Betrayal of the Child*. Trans. Hildegarde and Hunter Hannum. New York: Meridian, 1986.

----------. *For Your Own Good: Hidden Cruelty in Child-Rearing and the Roots of Violence*. Trans. Hildegarde and Hunter Hannum. New York: Farrar, Straus, Giroux, 1983.

Nader, Ralph. *Told You So: The Big Book of Weekly Columns*. New York: Seven Stories Press, 2013.

Nietzsche, Friedrich. *Beyond Good and Evil: Prelude to a Philosophy of the Future*. Trans. Walter Kaufmann. New York: Vintage, 1966.

----------. *The Gay Science*. Trans. Walter Kaufmann. New York: Vintage, 1974.

----------. *Thus Spake Zarathustra: A Book for All and None*. Trans. Walter Kaufmann. New York: Modern Library, 1995.

Orwell, George. *1984*. New York: Harcourt Brace, 2003.

Perkins, John. *Confessions of an Economic Hit Man*. New York: Plume, 2006.

Plato. *Five Dialogues: Euthyphro, Apology, Crito, Meno, Phaedo*. Trans. G.M.A. Grube. Indianapolis: Hackett, 1981.

----------. *The Republic*. Trans. Raymond Larson. Arlington Heights, IL: Harlan Davidson, 1979.

----------. *The Symposium*. Trans. Alexander Nehamas and Paul Woodruff. Indianapolis: Hackett, 1989.

Prins, Nomi. *It Takes a Pillage: An Epic Tale of Power, Deceit, and Untold Trillions*. Hoboken: John Wiley and Sons, 2011.

Reed, Ross Channing. *Love and Death: An Existential Theory of Addiction*. Bloomington, IN: Xlibris, 2009.

----------. *The Terror of the Simulacra* (trilogy). Salem, MO: Ozark Mountain Writers Guild, forthcoming.

Salinger, J. D. *The Catcher in the Rye*. New York: Back Bay Books, 2001.

Sartre, Jean-Paul.   *Being and Nothingness: A Phenomenological Essay on Ontology*. Trans. Hazel E. Barnes. New York: Washington Square Press, 1966.

----------. *Nausea*. Trans. Lloyd Alexander.   New York: New Directions, 1964.

Scahill, Jeremy. *Blackwater: The Rise of the World's Most Powerful Mercenary Army*. New York: Nation Books, 2008.

-----------. *Dirty Wars: The World Is A Battlefield*. New York; Nation Books, 2013.

Scheer, Robert. *The Great American Stickup: How Reagan   Republicans and Clinton Democrats Enriched Wall Street While Mugging Main Street*. New York: Nation Books, 2010.

Seneca. *The Stoic Philosophy of Seneca*. Trans. Moses Hadas. New York: W. W. Norton, 1958.

Sinclair, Upton. *The Jungle*. New York: Penguin Classics, 1986.

Smiley, Tavis and Cornel West. *The Rich and the Rest of Us: A Poverty Manifesto*. New York: SmileyBooks, 2012.

Steinbeck, John. *The Grapes of Wrath*. New York: Penguin Classics, 2006.

Stiglitz, Joseph E. *The Price of Inequality: How Today's Divided Society Endangers Our Future*. New York: W. W. Norton, 2012.

Stout, Martha. *The Sociopath Next Door*. New York: Broadway Books, 2005.

Thucydides. *History of the Peloponnesian War*. Ed. M. I. Finley. Trans. Rex Warner. New York: Penguin, 1972.

Taibbi, Matt. *The Great Derangement: A Terrifying True Story of War, Politics, and Religion at the Twilight of the American Empire*. New York: Spiegel and Grau, 2008.

----------. *Griftopia: A Story of Bankers, Politicians, and the Most Audacious Power Grab in American History*. New York: Spiegel and Grau, 2011.

West, Cornel. *Living and Loving Out Loud: A Memoir*. New York: SmileyBooks, 2009.

Winter. John Ellsworth. *Undoomed Warrior: The Strange Case of R. E. Lee and the "Gettysburg" Campaign*. Harrisburg, PA: Cadmus House, 2013.

Wolff, Richard D. *Capitalism Hits the Fan: The Global Economic   Meltdown and What to Do About It.* 2nd Revised Edition. Northampton, MA: Interlink Publishing Group, 2013.

----------. *Democracy at Work: A Cure for Capitalism.* Chicago: Haymarket Books, 2012.

Zinn, Howard. *A People's History of the United States.* New York: Perennial Classics, 2003.

ORGANIZATIONS, WEBSITES AND PERIODICALS

American Civil Liberties Union: www.aclu.org
Amnesty International: www.amnesty.org
American Student Assistance: www.asa.org
Board of Governors of the Federal Reserve System:
        www.federalreserve.gov
Bureau of Investigative Journalism:
        www.thebureauinvestigates.com
Catholic Worker Movement:
www.catholicworker.org
Center for Constitutional Rights: www.ccrjustice.org
Center for Media and Democracy:
www.prwatch.org/cmd
CODEPINK: www.codepink.org
www.costofwar.com
Costs of War Project: www.costsofwar.org
www.democracynow.org
Demos: www.demos.org
www.earthship.com
Free Speech TV: www.freespeech.org

Harper's Magazine: http://harpers.org/
Human Rights Watch: www.hrw.org
www.icasualities.org
Institute for Policy Studies: www.ips-dc.org
International Socialist Review: www.isreview.org
www.iraqbodycount.org
Link TV: www.linktv.org
www.lovedeathaddiction.com
Mother Jones magazine: www.motherjones.com
The Nation magazine: www.thenation.com
www.philosophicalcounselingtoday.com
Rolling Stone magazine:
http://www.rollingstone.com/
Stanford Encyclopedia of Philosophy:
http://plato.stanford.edu
United States and World Population Clock:
www.census.gov/popclock
www.usdebtclock.org
Vanity Fair magazine: www.vanityfair.com
Veterans for Peace: www.veteransforpeace.org
Voices for Creative Nonviolence: www.vcnv.org
Wired magazine: http://www.wired.com/magazine/

FILMS

All Quiet on the Western Front
Blade Runner
Brazil
Capitalism: A Love Story
Catch-22
Children of Men
Citizen Koch
The Cove

A Crude Awakening: The Oil Crash
Departures
Dirty Wars
Doubt
The End of Poverty?
Escape From Suburbia
Eternal Sunshine of the Spotless Mind
Fuel
Garbage Warrior
GasLand
GasLand II
Green Zone
Gunner Palace
Hacking Democracy
Howard Zinn: You Can't Be Neutral
How Green Was My Valley
The Hurt Locker
Fast Food Nation
Food, Inc.
I, Robot
Idiocracy
Inside Job
Intolerance
Iraq for Sale
Iraq in Fragments
Lord of War
The Matrix
Mind the Gap
Minority Report
The Most Dangerous Man in America
Noam Chomsky: Rebel Without a Pause
No End in Sight
Pan's Labyrinth

The Queen of Versailles
Ralph Nader: An Unreasonable Man
The Road
Sicko
Solaris
Speaking Freely: Vol. 1: John Perkins
Swimming With Sharks
Taxi to the Dark Side
There Will Be Blood
This Film is Not Yet Rated
The Tillman Story
Uncovered: The War On Iraq
Unprecedented
Wall Street
Wall Street: Money Never Sleeps
War, Inc.
War Made Easy
Who Killed the Electric Car?
Why We Fight
Winter's Bone
WMD: Weapons of Mass Deception

20977285R00111

Made in the USA
Charleston, SC
01 August 2013